ISBN 978-1-333-52810-2
PIBN 10515835

1 MONTH OF
FREE
READING

at
www.ForgottenBooks.com

By purchasing this book you are eligible for one month membership to ForgottenBooks.com, giving you unlimited access to our entire collection of over 700,000 titles via our web site and mobile apps.

To claim your free month visit:
www.forgottenbooks.com/free515835

English
Français
Deutsche
Italiano
Español
Português

www.forgottenbooks.com

Mythology Photography **Fiction**
Fishing Christianity **Art** Cooking
Essays Buddhism Freemasonry
Medicine **Biology** Music **Ancient
Egypt** Evolution Carpentry Physics
Dance Geology **Mathematics** Fitness
Shakespeare **Folklore** Yoga Marketing
Confidence Immortality Biographies
Poetry **Psychology** Witchcraft
Electronics Chemistry History **Law**
Accounting **Philosophy** Anthropology
Alchemy Drama Quantum Mechanics
Atheism Sexual Health **Ancient History**
Entrepreneurship Languages Sport
Paleontology Needlework Islam
Metaphysics Investment Archaeology
Parenting Statistics Criminology
Motivational

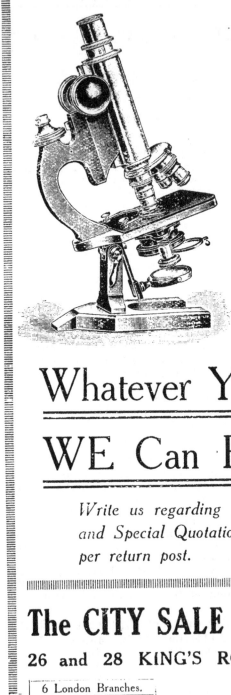

Here We Give
a Few Quotations
From Our List.

¶ Ross Microscope, rack focussing, fine adjustment, mechanical stage, vertical and horizontal movements, plane and concave mirrors, •one eye piece, $\frac{1}{8}$in. and 1in. objectives, inclinable to horizontal, in excellent condition   -   -   -   -   **£18 0 0**

¶ Ross Microscope, (binocular and monocular) mechanical stage, vertical and horizontal movements, actuated by rack adjustment, revolving movement, mechanical sub-stage vertical, horizontal and revolving movements, actuated rack and pinion, inclinable to the horizontal, with locking lever, 3-in. plane and concave mirrors, all movements, revolving diaphragm, fine adjustment, the binocular portion is fitted rack and pinion for adjustment of the eye pieces to the pupilary distance, brilliant illumination polariscope (with adjustment), compressarium achromatic condenser, 1-in. Lieberkuln four eye pieces, live box, $\frac{1}{8}$-in., $\frac{1}{4}$-in., $\frac{1}{2}$-in., $1\frac{1}{2}$-in., 2-in., 3-in., 4-in. objectives, equal to new, price **£37 10 0**

¶ Microscope by Beck, rack and pinion focussing, micrometer, fine adjustment revolving stage with all movements, long pull-out, total length 15$\frac{1}{2}$in., concave mirror, diaphragm dual objectives giving $\frac{1}{2}$-in. and 1-in. foci, also extra $\frac{1}{4}$-in. objectives, two eye pieces, stand inclinable to the horizontal, mahogany cabinet, price   -   -   -   -   -   **£5 10 0**

See Previous Page.

The CITY SALE & EXCHANGE
26 & 28 KING'S ROAD, Sloane Square,

| 6 London Branches. |

LONDON, S.W.3.

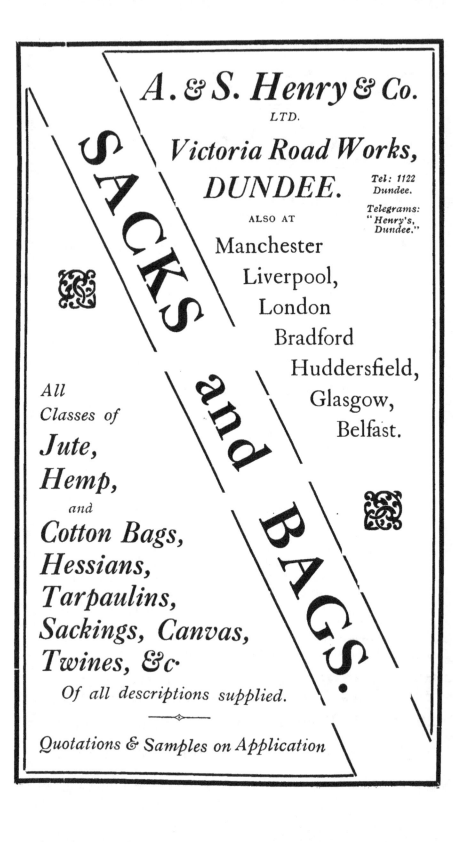

WHEAT AND THE FLOUR MILL.

A HANDBOOK FOR PRACTICAL FLOUR MILLERS.

The late

WHEAT AND THE
OUR MILL

A HANDBOOK FOR
PRACTICAL FLOUR MILLERS

BY THE LATE

EDWARD BRADFIELD

Editor of " Milling," Liverpool

A COLLECTION OF FUGITIVE PAPERS ON THE THEORY
OF MODERN FLOUR MILLING BY A
FORME

WITH A FOREWORD BY

ROBERT C. WINTER

Manager, Liverpool Grain Storage and Transit Co.

LIVERPOOL
THE NORTHERN PUBLISHING COMPANY, L

1920

WHEAT AND THE FLOUR MILL .

A HANDBOOK FOR PRACTICAL FLOUR MILLERS

BY THE LATE

EDWARD BRADFIELD

Editor of " Milling," Liverpool

A COLLECTION OF FUGITIVE PAPERS ON THE THEORY
AND PRACTICE OF MODERN FLOUR MILLING BY A
FORMER MILLER

WITH A FOREWORD BY

ROBERT C. WINTER

Manager, Liverpool Grain Storage and Transit Co.

———

LIVERPOOL :
THE NORTHERN PUBLISHING COMPANY, LIMITED.

———

1920

CONTENTS.

PUBLISHERS' NOTE.

The Proprietors of MILLING, in issuing this Collection of Papers by their late Editor, desire to acknowledge their indebtedness to :—Professor WM. JAGO, F.I.C., F.C.S. author of "The Technology of Bread-Making," for the chapter "The Bleaching of Flour" from a chemist's point of view; MR. JOHN KIRKLAND, of the Borough Polytechnic and author of "The Modern Baker," for the chapter "The Bleaching of Flour" from a baker's point of view; and Mr. F. E. TREHARNE, F.C.S., Director of Spillers' Milling and Associated Industries, Ltd., for the chapter "Chemistry and Physics as applied to Milling." Without these contributions it would have been impossible to complete the work which was interrupted by the untimely death of Mr. BRADFIELD.

A FOREWORD.

Our small library of Milling Technology can be divided into three groups of books; each group indicates the metier of the author, mechanics, chemistry, or practice. The last-named group is the least prolific, and to it this book belongs.

EDWARD BRADFIELD was a miller, and never confused his claims with those of the chemist or the engineer. He saw that his craftsmanship provided in itself a whole subject, and he used up the zeal and energy of his youth in an effort to focus for to-day all the light which he could throw, or which had been thrown, on that subject. He was old enough to be something of a seer with a thought for the long, slow road we had traversed, and an outlook for the future; he was young enough to be something of a revolutionary with a laugh and a shout for each new plunge that might precipitate some healthy change, or break a shackle of the past. When such a man writes a book, it is worth a young man's while to read it, even though, as in this case, it is only concerned with a record—a focus, as it were—of the craft sense at the time of writing.

His best work was done for the apprentice. In the pages of *Milling* and elsewhere he used his undoubted talent to clear the way for the young miller, particularly, I believe, for the man whose education had not wholly been made good by the opportunities afforded in sweeping flour mill floors in the beginning of his teens. This book was meant for these men in its conception; in its completion it will be helpful to all.

May I use this honour and privilege of mine to emphasise, as the author would have done, the need for acute practical observation along with study. To turn to page 8, say, and then to describe Red Winter wheat as red, mild, dry, long, etc., is *not* study, however far it may go towards circumventing the purpose of examinations. In such foolishness lies the root of the controversy over the "practical" men and the maligned "theorists." In this instance a book is published to suggest Edward Bradfield's words and terms for certain characteristics and observations. If other words and terms are found which more adequately convey the true conceptions, then alter them without a moment's hesitation. But before you have studied Red Winter wheat (in handfuls, not in books), you must read the wheat as a traveller reads his map, or a surgeon anatomy. Further, in a field of so vast a scope as ours the man who reads and finds nothing to alter is likely to prove the slave of some primitive text book. Read this book then (and all good books for that matter) by the safe sure light of your daily working experience, so that it will lead you to craftsmanship, and not to platitudes.

Know your wheats; know them so that from each day's handful you may extract your own classifications with assurance; know them so that when changes are made, you are not dependent upon your recollections of printed or oral matter for your subsequent reputation. Know the operations, their causes and effects, by experiment, by wrong-doing if need be, for in technics the end does justify the means. Do not be afraid to tackle the simple chemistry of your subject rather than be tied all your life to descriptions of tests, which, however cleverly written, either do not convey to your mind anything like the truth, or, at best, tell only a fraction of it.

Had my friend lived to see the publication of these articles I know that he would have made haste to salute the friends who helped him to glean and garner his information. Happily, they know that too and I can safely leave the matter so.

R. C. WINTER.

Liverpool,
   March, 1920.

INTRODUCTION

The birth of corn milling is lost in the mists of antiquity. From time immemorial, at any rate in Europe and in Western Asia, man has eaten of the ground products of cereals, of which wheat has naturally been the chief. Nor do our records cease even when we get back beyond the confines of historical knowledge. Archæologists have made discoveries which go to show that in some, at any rate, of the distant ages which existed before our earliest purely historical records, man lived, grew wheat, and reduced it to flour, or more accurately, meal.

Wheat unreduced and uncooked does not make a wholesome human food, and the fact that it was looked upon as a staple food must always betoken the existence of a considerable amount of knowledge and civilisation on the part of those prehistoric men whom we know to have used it. How wheat came to be cultivated, in what way it was found that reducing and cooking made it into an ideal human food, or how long the cereals took to attain the position we find them occupying in our earliest records, there are, of course, no means of ascertaining. The Romans ascribed the knowledge of the value of corn to the goddess Ceres. According to Virgil the legend ran that man first subsisted on nuts and then on acorns, and then Ceres had pity on him and taught him the art of husbandry and thus gave him wheat and bread. It is an interesting, if perhaps not strictly relevant reflection that in the evolution of man, the order given in the legend quoted is probably the correct one, and that the primæval men lived first on the wild fruits of the earth, and only at a much later date learned how to till the soil, and grow wheat, and cook the meal made from it, is a suggestion quite in accordance with the latest theories of evolutionary science. It is also an instance of how the early legends of a people awakening into civilization, though glossed over with their rude superstitions and mythology, often contain the elements of truth.

Side by side with the evidences of the use of cultivation of wheat come evidences and records of the methods of reducing the wheat—in fact of the first mills. It is established quite certainly that to the pestle and mortar we must look for the earliest form of mill. In the classical and other early writings, and in the translations made from them, the references to mills have often been obscured by the prepossessions of the writer or translator, and mills of a more advanced type than they actually possessed have been ascribed to early races. Specimens of these forerunners of the mill have been found first among the discoveries relating to the now submerged prehistoric lake villages of Switzerland, and of later date in Egypt, Asia Minor, Italy, England and elsewhere.

Following the pestle and mortar came the saddleback mill. In this mill the bottom stone was broad and of fair length, hollowed in the middle and of considerable area. On it the corn to be ground was placed. The grinding stone was a long round stone, not unlike a thick rolling pin, and this was rubbed—not rolled—up and down on the wheat. It may be said in this case that the grinding always was done by slaves and usually by women.

Next came the hand quern. In this case we have the prototype of the modern mill stone. The quern, or hand mill, was universal throughout the world for a long period and practically all the writers in ancient, classical and Biblical writings, when referring to mills had this type of mill in their minds. The quern was constructed in a fashion rudely similar to a modern pair of stones. The bottom stone was fixed, and at the top there was the runner. It was worked, of course, by manual—female—labour, and as considerable force was required to turn the mill, and as the operation of grinding was necessarily tedious and wearisome, two women—as the phrase goes—generally were sent together to grind at the mill and worked alternately. As for the sifting or flour dressing, a primitive coarse hand sieve of pierced parchment or intertwined grass was the only bolter, although one or two references have been somewhat strained to show that quite fine meal was required at an early date. After the hand quern was developed, came the cattle driven mills and the mills that were turned by numbers of slaves working together. These mills marked a distinct mechanical advance in the history of mill construction, but even so, the cattle mills could grind but slowly and were far behind the first power mills.

About the origin of the purely mechanically driven mill there exists a good deal of doubt.* Without going into details, it would seem that the first water mill was invented in Greece somewhere about the year 120 B.C. by Mithridates. It is interesting to note that the earliest form of water motor was a wheel lying horizontally with an upright vertical shaft driving straight on to the runner stone. It, of course, pierced the bed stone and was fitted to the upper runner stone. The water wheel itself was but a simple contrivance. A number of open, small, straight blades fixed in the end of the vertical spindle of the mill, a small falling stream of water, brought from the main river in a wooden trough, falling on to the blades of the wheel, such was the original water wheel.

About sixty years later came the vertical water wheel. This was invented in Italy, and the honour of being the inventor falls to Vitruvius, who lived just before the beginning of the Christian era. He wrote a book on mechanical inventions, and in it he gives a description of the water mill he had invented. In his mill, which was in several ways an improvement upon the Greek water mill, the wheel was vertical, the blades (buckets were not thought of) went right across the width of the narrow wheel, and the shaft was geared to the upright shaft which drove the stone.

After the invention of the Roman water wheel, progress in the art of mechanical milling seems practically to have ceased. In the dark ages which followed the downfall of the Roman Empire, very few improvements were attempted in the construction of flour mills, so that when at the commencement of the Middle Ages there are again definite records the milling trade is found to be in a not very different state from that in which it was at the end of the fourth century.

In the Domesday book there is a comprehensive list of the mills in many of the counties of England and a number of existing country mills can, without much difficulty, trace the existence of their mills right back to that early survey.

In the Middle Ages the mill was one of the appanages of the manor in which it happened to be situated. The lord owned the mill, the miller was his tenant and the former could and did compel the tenants to have all their grain ground at the estate mill. The universal custom was for each man to bring his own grain to be ground. This the miller was bound to do, and for payment he was allowed to retain a certain fixed proportion of the grist and this was known as the " toll," or in the aggregate as the " multure," and it varied in proportion from a thirteenth to a twenty-fourth of the total grist. The amount for each mill was fixed by law and custom as interpreted by the local lord of the manor; in no case could the miller alter it, he remained bound to his mill, paying a heavy rent in the form of services to the lord, the servant of all the tenants, unable by his wit or his work to add to his profits, he was not in an enviable position. Nor were millers commonly held in good repute; on what appear to be the slenderest foundations, if indeed there be any, there grew up in feudal England a traditional prejudice against the miller. His honesty was arraigned until the lack of it became proverbial. The whole position of the miller during the feudal period is ably summed up in the most brilliant passage of their book, by Bennett and Elton, in the " History of Corn Milling," a work which everyone who is interested in the early and mediæval history of the milling trade is recommended to read.

The student finds in his researches that only by slow degrees did improvements come into the trade until very recently indeed. It is, however, interesting to note that in some cases we find customs born out of due time. Thus, in the middle of the sixteenth century we find a number of Paris millers subjecting the wheat to two or three successive grindings in order to increase their yield of flour. They were also accustomed to buy bran from other millers, pass it through the stones, and recover some of the flour left on it. This foreshadowing of the principle of gradual reduction was, however, not due to any attempt to better the flour, nor were any efforts made to separate the middlings from the bran stock in the second or subsequent grindings. The sole object sought was a long yield of flour. The practice was for a long time kept secret by the few millers who used it, and even when it became known the custom never appears to have become in any way general.

A reference to the early laws and customs of milling, however brief, can hardly be made without some allusion to the millers' ancient " privileges " and " rights." It has been shown that in the Middle Ages the miller was encumbered with laws and ties. In return each mediæval mill had its " soke " or privileges. The chief of these consisted in the water rights—which remain in many cases to this day —and the monopoly it had in its own manor; thus any manorial mill could, and generally did, prevent any other mill from being built within the manor; or the tenants from getting their corn ground without it. This custom remained in many cases after the miller was freed from the restraint of the more irksome dues and services owed to the lord, and thus in not a few cases through the seventeenth and eighteenth centuries the mill was a source of great profit to the miller, who often became a rich man. When, moreover, the custom of buying wheat and selling flour grew up towards the close of the eighteenth century, the profits which were made were enormous in comparison with those of the present day, and indeed at that time and in the first decade or two of the nineteenth century, flour milling probably became a more profitable calling to the bulk of the members of the trade than it had been before, or perhaps has been since.

During the sixteenth, seventeenth and the first three-quarters of the eighteenth centuries, the technical improvements that were made consisted only in better and more refined fittings and better balanced and more easily adjustable stones. In 1774, however, the first steam engine to drive a flour mill was built by Boulton & Watt, and installed in the Albion Mills, Westminster, a mill in which were about thirty pairs of stones. The engine was not a complete success, but it inaugurated a mighty change in mill power. Oliver Evans, an American, who lived from 1756 to 1819, demands a few lines, for this man has the distinction of having invented the elevator and conveyor—or at least he first adapted them for use in flour mills. He designed a mill which was entirely automatic in action and he seems also to have had in his mind the possibilities of economical and mechanical grain handling, for he says in one of his advertisements that "right from the hold of the ship to the flour sack, handling by manual labour has now been made unnecessary." Evans was born in too early a generation, for although a number of mills on his system were set to work in America and a few in England, his ideas never received the encouragement they deserved. English mill engineers who lived about the same period as Evans, were not behind in improvement, as the old records of mills fitted up by Philip Williams, also by Fairburn fifty years later, amply set forth.

Mention of the two latter pioneer millwrights—as milling engineers were formerly called—leads to the consideration of the stone mill as it existed in England in the middle of last century, when it may be said to have attained to its full importance and glory. Ever since the introduction of steam in this country, improvements in every detail of the stone mills had been effected until they attained a pitch of perfection that would have seemed impossible two generations previously. In these days of huge modern mills it may be thought by a few of the younger men that the stone millers of last century were lacking in skill compared with that of their successors, the roller millers, and to underestimate the perfection of equipment which those mills contained is often another inaccurate view taken of stone milling. Such ideas are very far from being correct. Of the ten thousand flour mills which existed in England during the middle period of the last century, those driven by water power turned out the largest quantity of flour. In the big towns there were a few steam mills with as many as forty or fifty pairs of wheat stones, but the average steam mill would only have six pairs, while in the populous high or flat lands there were windmills without number and with from two to four pairs of stones each, only half that number being used for wheat grinding. The average water-driven mill contained perhaps four or six pairs of wheat stones and two Peak stones. The scheme of the mills was simple. English wheat formed the predominant part of the mixture. As a consequence it needed but little cleaning and in many—perhaps most—mills a separator and scourer were the only machines used. The wheat was stored in sacks or on floors. When required for mixing the grain was rebagged, and the several sorts shot, sack by sack, in the required proportion, into the dirty wheat bin immediately above the screens. After the grain had been lain in the dirty wheat bin till it had become homogenous and had been through the single "smutter" it was shot into the grinding bin over the "burr" stones— Derbyshire Peak stone being used for grinding coarse grain—and half the millers' art—and it was an art—was comprised in laying out and dressing the stone. Properly to lay out a stone; to attain the absolute balance; to mark out the quarters, lands, and furrows and, finally, to give the requisite fineness of dress to the surface, required a skill and judgment, and steadiness of hand and eye, of no mean order, and the old stone millers rightly prided themselves on the quality of their work. A good stoneman could put in the lands as many as 20 cracks to the inch. In all cases the top was the runner stone. The adjustment of the stones demanded at least as much skill as that required to set a line of rolls. In a few of the large town mills automatic methods were in operation and the meal from the stones was conveyed to the dressing machines by elevators and the meal dressed at once —though even in those cases there was usually some provision for cooling the meal. But in the majority of mills the warm meal fell into a bin, was shovelled into sacks by the miller and left perhaps for some days to cool. Then, when the time came for dressing, the meal was fed into either wire covered cylinders or long, round, slowly-moving, silk covered reels and the flour and offals sacked off. Altogether, the mid-Victorian millers were men of substance and men of skill.

Then came the changes. "High grinding," "gradual reduction" and the "roller system," one after the other, came to revolutionise the trade. The flour was greatly improved by the new methods and the trade of stone millers was decimated. The new methods allowed the brittle stony wheats then coming into fame to be made into excellent flour which the stone millers could not equal. Yet many of them, who clung to the traditional system which had brought them fame, wealth and honour, made heroic efforts to stay the onslaught, but failed. A few never had any doubt that the new methods had come to conquer. This historical sketch of the progress of the milling trade is necessarily brief, but the writer thinks he has brought the principal changes to notice. It must suffice now to say that while it is impossible to do anything but admire the science and engineering skill, and mechanical triumphs which are to be seen in every modern mill, and to admire also the genius and industry of the present generation of the millers of the United Kingdom which have put them in the front rank of the millers of the World, yet at the same time it would be ungenerous and unworthy to withhold from that former generation of millers, which under the old stone system established their craft as one of the most honourable of industries, the praise which is their due. But they have gone; and for the steadily moving, easily prosperous times of forty and fifty years ago, there is now an unparalleled stress of competition among the members of the trade. With that, the writer is not concerned for the moment, but is content to record the fact that the very stress of modern competition has led to many of the mechanical and economical improvements which have made British and Irish mills to be the best equipped in the World. Finally, it is but just to say that the credit for some of this progress must be given those German and Swiss engineers, who have brought out many improvements, which the millers of the United Kingdom have not been slow in adopting.

THE WORLD'S WHEAT.

THE STRENGTH FACTORS

CLIMATE. HARVESTS. VARIETIES.

Wheat has always held the premier place in the food economy of the most civilised races of the world, and during many centuries, until quite recent times, the failure of the wheat crop in any important country was the precursor of suffering and famine. This cereal has held the position as the staple food of the most energetic, and we think we may add, the most intelligent races of mankind ever since the time of which we have record, while, indeed, in prehistoric times there are evidences now to show that wheat was cultivated and ground into flour or meal on quite a general scale. In these prehistoric times it seems probable that the grain was ground into a rude kind of meal and was baked into a rough form of unleavened bread.

As a result of the universal demand for wheaten bread, this cereal is now grown in every country of the temperate zone, but in the geographical distributions of the world's crop there have been remarkable changes during the last half century. During this period many countries previously self-supporting have become importers, while others where wheat was hardly grown at all have become large exporters. Mention need only now be made of the phenomenal and unprecedented increases in the production of Canada, Argentina and Australia, countries, which at the beginning of the era named produced a bare sufficiency for their own needs, but at the present time export a total quantity of some tens of millions of quarters. The consumption of wheaten bread and flour products has also become more general in those countries where rye was formerly the staple food, and at the present

B

time we find even rice-consuming countries, such as China and Japan, importing an ever-increasing quantity of wheaten flour. In England, almost alone of all countries, wheat cultivation has largely decreased, so that to-day there is merely an average production of seven million quarters of wheat to compare with the fifteen million quarters that were grown yearly half-a-century ago. The causes of this decline —coincident in time with the rise of roller milling—have been solely economic, and though the effect on the milling trade has been considerable cannot here be considered in any detail. One quotation, however, from the *Corn Trade Year Book* of 1904, may be given to indicate one of the root causes of the decline. "It is said that the Italian peasant in Argen tina, in a mud hut, can rear a large family of children on what he grows himself upon his newly acquired allotment, for his wants are practically nil in the first two years of his struggle, being confined to a little fuel and an odd garment or two. Ten months out of the twelve he leads an idle life, but at seed-time and harvest he, his wife and his children down to the very toddlers, work from daybreak until nightfall and on moonlight nights they may sometimes be seen toiling away far into the night at the ingathering of the harvest. Under such circumstances, is it likely that the British farmer can compete when he has appearances to keep up and rent and taxes to pay? Science and a good situation are worth much, but they can be hardly reckoned as a set-off against pauper labour on a virgin soil." The above quotation has been given, because it very forcibly illustrates one of the factors in the decline of English wheat culture, that has not always been sufficiently taken into account. With the other aspects of this economic problem, or with the remedies that have been proposed it would be out of place now to deal. Suffice it to say that though since the above quotation was written (1904) times have been better for the farmers, the area under wheat cultivation in England has not materially increased, nor at the present does there appear any likelihood of its so doing; though during the war the area under wheat in England in 1918 rose to approximately 2,790,000 acres, and the yield to 11,647,000 quarters. But the above is by the way; still the subject is one which considerably affects the milling trade.

The inevitable consequence of this decline of British wheat production has been a corresponding increase in the importation of wheat, so that at the present time the British miller, among all the millers of the world, is the most cosmopolitan, and invades the markets of every country buying where he most profitably may. As a result he has to mill a number of wheats differing from each other most radically in every respect. These must be conditioned, blended and milled to produce a regular, dependable flour. It is thus easy to see how important is a study of these wheats and a knowledge of the results that may be expected from them and their true economic value. This knowledge can be, of course, only fully obtained after long experience, but every young miller can acquire, by his combined reading and observation, a fair knowledge of the properties of the chief wheats of the world. The value of this knowledge can hardly be over-estimated.

Pekar, who immortalised himself by his flour test, once stated that there were eight hundred known varieties of wheat in the world. As this estimate was made some considerable time ago, and new varieties are continually being produced by agricultural experts, it is not too much to say that at the present time there must be altogether at least a thousand known varieties. Not all, nor even the greater number, fortunately, come to this country to be separately marketed, and in the case of foreign wheats arriving in this country millers usually rely on the commercial grades and names, and only occasionally—as in the case as to whether "Velvet Chaff" should grade as No. 1 Northern Duluth—do they concern themselves with the actual name or even variety of the wheat they buy. Here only those grades and varieties of wheat can be considered which are found—or recently have been found— on English markets, together with a few well-known foreign varieties which are not seen in England. Even so, there will be nearly a hundred varieties to take into account.

A number of broad classifications into which wheat may be divided occur to the mind. Wheats may be classified as to their colour, i.e., either red, white or yellow; and their strength—strong, medium, weak; or the colour of the flour made from them—white, yellow-tinted, grey; or their structure, flinty, hard, mellow, soft; or their district or country of origin, together with a commercial title. The latter is the most general method—and will here be adopted.

The highest-priced wheats are almost always of the strongest varieties. Next come the wheats which will produce the whitest flour, together with a fine bloom and brilliancy. Thus the best spring wheats of the United States and Canada usually head the price list, while, on the other hand, Australians, on account of their excellent properties of colour and bloom, stand high. Speaking generally, however, strength is the best asset for any wheat. Exactly what determines or constitutes " strength " in wheat is not even now quite certain. It has long been known that it is on the gluten that the strength of a wheat depends, and for some little time it has been recognised that quality, as opposed to the quantity of the gluten, is the determining factor. The chemical aspect of the subject, however, can be treated elsewhere, and the general factors which determine the milling qualities of the wheat grown are not difficult to discover. They are three in number and to adopt Mr. Voller's nomenclature as being the best and briefest, are, climate, pedigree and soil. The importance of the first two of these factors is almost obvious, that of the third must not be overlooked, as will be seen presently.

The strongest wheats then are found in the spring wheat lands of the United States, the Canadian North-west, Russia and Hungary. Leaving for the moment the question of seed, we find that in each case the climatic conditions are almost identical, while except perhaps in one instance, the respective soils are of a similar nature. In each case there is a " continental " climate. That is to say, the winter is long and severe, with a heavy snowfall, the spring is short, mild and damp, the summer is hot and the harvesting period is dry and warm. It would seem that the cold is in some way needed to develop the " strength " properties of the gluten, while the summer heat aids and completes this process. The result in each case is a fine, hard wheat of great strength and the best possible gluten. It has been suggested that the thick " snow blanket " through the winter has in some way an effect upon the seed-bed. With regard to the soil, we find that on the prairie lands of the States and Canada and on the steppes of Russia, the grain is sown in soil of unique quality. This soil in many cases consists almost wholly of decayed vegetable matter. This is very rich in nitrogenous and nitrogen producing and giving substances. And it is on these latter that the strength of the gluten largely depends. Consequently, when appraising the different factors which go to produce great strength in the wheats mentioned, the nature of the soil must be taken into sufficient account. As corroborative evidence of this effect, the oft-expressed opinion of many millers that the United States spring wheats are not now so strong as they were some five and twenty years ago may be quoted. This belief is very widespread and assuming it to be true, it may be pointed out that in the States comparatively little virgin ground has been broken during the last few years, while a system of farming exhaustive to the ground has been practised. Under these circumstances it is not unreasonable to suppose that some of the great nitrogenous resources of that soil have been used up to the detriment of the gluten, and, consequently, loss of strength to the wheat. In Canada, on the other hand, and to a lesser degree, Russia, fresh ground has continually been broken, richer lands found, while in Canada, at any rate, more farseeing systems of farming have been practised. As a result, No. 1 Hard Manitoba has gradually gained in reputation and to-day is probably fully the equal, if not the superior, of any other wheat in the world as regards strength.

A consideration of the strong wheats leads to the further conclusion that strength is not at all an inherent feature of wheat. Rather it would appear to be a characteristic only developed under domestication and a special environment.

In support of this we may note two facts among others, first that wheats, more or less deficient in strength, may be found growing under all kinds of different conditions and, second. that strong wheats are always inclined to lose—to a greater or less degree—their outstanding characteristics when transplanted to altered conditions of climate and soil. The special case of wheats produced by the Home-grown Wheat Committee will be dealt with later.

As we have mentioned above, wheats lacking in strength grow under widely differing conditions. Thus, many English sorts, Oregon, New Zealand and Egyptian wheats, all grow under widely differing conditions both of soil and climate, yet with one result at any rate in common. The qualities of English soil and the vagaries of the English climate are too well known to need mention. On the Pacific Coast there is generally hard silicious soil, which gives the grain an artificial hardness, having no connection with strength, the climate is warm and dry; in New Zealand the climate resembles the English, but is a little drier, in Egypt the soil consists of mud over sand, the worst possible for wheat growing, while the heat is often excessive and the rainfall is almost non existent. It can be seen then that weakness is produced not so much by any positive characteristics as by the absence of those essentials of strength to which allusion has been made before. Other features of these wheats will be given in their proper place.

Perhaps mainly for the benefit of the young millers who will read these lines, we may now proceed to a detailed consideration of the milling qualities of the various wheats of the world. Two forewords may be given. First, a student ought not to let his knowledge stop at the very brief notes that will follow, he should see to it that his observation and his experience of the wheats in his own mill are continually adding to his knowledge of both their positive and relative value. Secondly, it must, at this and every stage, be borne in mind that the crucial test for both flour and wheat will occur only in the oven, and that the loaf of bread is the criterion by which all flour must be finally judged.

American Spring Wheats.

Foremost among the wheats of the United States are the Spring wheats. The term includes the Duluth, Milwaukee, Chicago and Minnesota groups and of these No. 1 Northern Duluth is, perhaps, the best. All wheat, however, grading No. 1 Northern Spring is among the best of its kind and for many years the best Duluth had the reputation of being the strongest variety in the world, being rivalled only by the choicest Theis and Saxonska, but at the present time there is little to choose for strength between the choicest Spring and Manitoban wheats—the preference, if any, being in favour of the latter. The best Spring wheat is red, lustrous, hard and plump, with small well-filled grains, having a high natural weight, yielding a fair percentage of flour of great strength and good colour. A loaf made from this flour will be very lofty and big, with an excellent texture and a good colour. The flavour also will be fair, though not equal to a loaf made from Winter wheat flour, or the two mixed. The crust will be almost the only point in the loaf calling for real criticism—this tends to be tough—the great feature of the loaf, however, will be its size. In addition to these characteristics, flour from Spring wheat has a considerable water-absorbing capacity, so that a large number of loaves per sack may be obtained.

Impurities are few and not difficult to extract, consisting chiefly of oats, barley, cockle, buckwheat, small seeds and dust. No. 2 Spring sometimes comes to England—the properties are similar to No. 1, with a slight inferiority in all respects. The difference between the two top grades of Spring wheat is rather more marked than that between No. 1 and No. 2 Northern Manitoban. Impurities also exist in greater proportion. U.S.A. grades, below No. 2 Spring, are not shipped to England and need not be considered now, being very similar to the lower grades of Manitobans, which will be referred to later.

" Spring " wheat is usually sown in April and harvested in August and September. The condition of soil and climate under which it is grown have already been referred to.

American Winter Wheats.

These wheats, which rank next after the Spring wheats in importance to the export trade, comprise another group of fine varieties. They are grown in the middle and eastern States where the climate is rather damper and milder, and generally more equable than in the Spring wheat lands.

Red Winter is the premier variety of the group. As its name implies it is a red wheat, mild and dry in structure, long and large of berry, with a tough, thick bran, but the size of the grains often differs considerably in a single sample. The flour will be of medium strength and the yield high and colour good. A loaf baked from this flour alone will be of medium size, good colour, very sweet flavour, with a nice texture and excellent crust, but usually not yielding so many loaves per sack as Spring wheat. Its special point is its sweet flavour, which is only surpassed by flour made from very good English.

Impurities in good samples are few, chiefly seeds, cockle, oats, maize and dust, and sometimes garlic. Hard Winter wheat from Kansas and the middle States arrives in fair quantities in this country. It resembles Red Winter, but is much harder, of a rather ricey texture, is not so red in colour, is stronger, but not so well flavoured, produces a splendid crust in the loaf, and a good coloured flour; it does not yield quite so well as Red Winter.

Western Winter is another kindred variety of medium hardness, but not quite so valuable a quality as Kansas Winter. It tends also to be irregular and is not so generally favoured among millers.

The impurities of both the latter varieties are somewhat more abundant, consisting usually of small seeds, oats, barley and dust.

" Winter " wheat is usually sown in October and harvested in the following June.

Michigan grows a white variety which has not been exported to England in recent years. It is said to be of a good average quality and suitable for mixing purposes, with properties similar in a good many respects to those of English wheat, generally soft and weak; it is a useful variety with which to fill up a mixture.

Pacific Coast Varieties.

We next come to a consideration of the Pacific Coast varieties. The chief of these arriving in this country are Blue Stem, Walla Walla, Oregon and Californian. The climate of the Pacific Coast is hot and dry. After the harvest in some districts the grain, after being cut and bagged, is allowed to lie in the fields for weeks together; in short, until it is convenient to move it. The soil is not rich, but thin and sandy. There is no snow or cold to harden and improve the gluten properties, and consequently the wheats are all of a dry, brittle nature and very weak.

The Blue Stem variety is white, with medium-sized berries of rather an elongated shape, is mild in structure and dry, absorbing water quickly during the conditioning process. It obtains its name from the colour of its straw, which has a peculiar blueish tinge. The yield of flour is high and the colour of the latter is good, while its strength is moderate. There is, however, a tendency toward a rather dry, insipid taste in the loaf. Samples of this wheat are usually very clean, the impurities generally consisting only of ordinary cockle, oats, barley and stones.

Walla Walla is another variety inferior in quality, as a rule, to either of the foregoing Pacific wheats. It is yellow, brittle, dry and ricey and not of a particularly pleasing appearance. The flour yield is only fair and it is very weak and yellow, and requires bleaching. The yellow tint imparted to the flour is the most striking characteristic of all the Walla wheats. Walla Walla takes water as quickly as any wheat in the world, except, perhaps, Australian. The impurities are oats, barley, stones, dirt and small seeds.

Red Walla is also grown; it is a brittle red wheat and very dry, yielding a flour that sometimes is " as yellow as a guinea," otherwise similar to the white wheat above.

Oregon—This is a very bold white wheat, having a good yield of flour, but its quality, except as regards its whiteness, is very moderate, for it is one of the weakest varieties known. It is the mildest of the Pacific wheats and has large oval berries. Oregon, like Walla, is much weaker than Blue Stem, which is the strongest and best of the Pacific sorts. Oregon wheat is fairly free from impurities and appears to a non-practical eye as a very superior kind, but it belies its appearance.

Californian is a dry, ricey, white wheat, good looking, with large, well-filled grains. It gives a good percentage of flour and ranks high among the world's wheats for colour, but has poor strength. Impurities are similar to the other Pacific wheats. There used frequently to be found a pungent smelling, small, round seed known as melilot, which would give the flour a most unpleasant odour that could be detected even in the bread. This remained, even though the wheat, when ground, was free from melilot and it was only after thorough washing and conditioning became general that the effects of this small seed could be overcome. Californian arrives only in small quantities in this country now, but it is a useful sort to add to a mixture when obtainable.

The above concludes the list of Pacific Coast wheats; it will be seen that they are valuable for their colour and good yielding properties, but of no account at all either for flavour or strength. These white wheats are in great demand in Ireland, especially Blue Stem which' next to Australian wheat, is the most sought after variety in that country. They form a useful group for port millers, using all foreign wheats, but are not usually bought by inland millers who have a supply of native wheats, which are cheaper and often better. Of late years there has been a diminishing quantity shipped to the United Kingdom, partly on account of increased local flour production, and partly because of the greatly increased demand from the Orient.

There is also a considerable quantity of Durum wheat grown in the United States, but, as its home is in South Eastern Europe, a consideration of its properties will be left until the varieties of that region are dealt with. Durum has only been cultivated in the States since 1898, and is grown chiefly in the semi-arid regions of the Western States. There it has become popular with the farmers, who grow it as a "safety" or "insurance" crop, and the annual production now amounts to about 40,000,000 bushels.

U. S. A.

PRODUCTION OF WHEAT.

Harvested June to August.	Autumn sown.	Spring sown.	Total.
1910	*54,268,000	25,122,000	79,390,000
1911	53,832,000	23,835,000	77,667,000
1912	49,989,000	*41,293,000	91,283,000
1913	65,445,000	29,977,000	95,422,000
1914	85,623,000	25,753,000	111,376,000

EXPORTS BY U.S.A. TO ALL DESTINATIONS,

According to Official American Returns.

Season ended 30th June.	Wheat. Qrs., 480 lbs.	Flour. Sacks, 280 lbs.	Total as Wheat. Qrs., 480 lbs.
1911	2,711,000	7,109,000	8,634,000
1912	3,364,000	7,687,000	9,770,000
1913	11,156,000	7,940,000	17,773,000
1914	11,286,000	8,208,000	18,126,000
1915	31,916,000	11,178,000	41,230,000

IMPORTS OF U.S.A. WHEAT AND FLOUR BY THE U.K.

Season ended 31st July.	Wheat. Qrs., 480 lbs.	Flour. Sacks, 280 lbs.	Total as Wheat. Qrs., 480 lbs.
1911	2,024,000	2,050,000	3,733,000
1912	3,888,000	1,826,000	5,410,000
1913	6,888,000	2,156,000	8,684,000
1914	6,840,000	2,194,000	8,669,000
1915	9,885,000	2,958,000	12,351,000

The above are British Board of Trade figures and are not to be relied upon owing to the peculiar manner in which they are compiled.

U. S. A.

IMPORTS INTO U.K.

Season ended 31st July.	Wheat. Qrs., 480 lbs.	Flour. Sacks, 280 lbs.	Total as Wheat. Qrs., 480 lbs.
1911	2,024,500	2,050,400	3,733,200
1912	3,887,900	1,826,200	5,409,700
1913	6,887,800	2,156,000	8,684,500
1914	6,840,100	2,194,200	8,668,600
1915	9,885,500	2,958,100	12,350,600

WHEAT AND THE FLOUR MILL.

U. S. A.

CROP—WHEAT.

Harvested July/August.	Winter.	Spring.	Total.
1910	54,267,800	25,122,300	79,390,100
1911	53,832,000	23,835,300	77,667,300
1912	49,989,900	41,293,500	91,283,400
1913	65,445,100	29,977,400	95,422,500
1914	85,623,800	25,753,300	111,377,100

U. S. A.

EXPORTS OF WHEAT & FLOUR.—OFFICIAL U.S.A. RETURN.

Season ended 30th June.	Wheat. Qrs., 480 lbs.	Flour. Sacks, 280 lbs.	Total as Wheat. Qrs., 480 lbs.
1911	2,710,600	7,108,700	8,634,500
1912	3,364,400	7,687,400	9,770,600
1913	11,156,300	7,940,400	17,773,300
1914	11,286,000	8,208,500	18,126,400
1915	31,916,000	11,177,900	41,230,900

Canadian Wheats.

The Canadian wheats next claim consideration. Canada is at the present time the most important, though not quite the largest, wheat exporter to the United Kingdom, and, as both Russia and the United States have in recent years been irregular and undependable exporters, is our chief source of strong wheat. The expansion of Canadian wheat production and exports has been one of the most notable features in the world's commerce during the last two decades. Thus, while in the ten years ending 1899 the average yearly wheat exports from Canada to all countries were but slightly over 1,000,000 quarters, in 1912 the exports to the United Kingdom alone amounted to nearly 6,000,000 quarters, the total export being about 12,000,000 quarters. In the second year of the war Canada exported 36,000,000 quarters of Wheat and flour combined. This expansion has synchronised with the diminution in the exports of Spring wheat from the United States, so that Canadian wheat is now the staple strong wheat of British millers. Even a short survey of the conditions, opportunities and prospects of the Canadian Northwest cannot be attempted

12

here, and it must suffice to say that, for all practical purposes, there is an almost unlimited area still awaiting cultivation. The methods of farming are superior to those which
have been practised in the States, with the result that the
quality of the wheat produced has been maintained. Inten-
sive and mixed farming is on the increase, while the opening
of the Panama Canal will facilitate transport, stimulate
production and open out yet another vast arable area in the
Far West. It is difficult to see a limit to Canadian expansion
—the one thing needful is an adequate supply of labour, and
as that becomes available we may expect to see ever increasing quantities of wheat shipped to the Old World from the
land of the Maple Leaf.

Another reason, though perhaps a minor one, for the
great increase in Canadian exports, has been the manner in
which the Canadian Government has organised carefully the
grading system, so that the buyer always knows for what
wheat he is paying. Uncertainty as to the quality of the
wheat contracted for has done much in the past to curtail the
business of several exporting countries, notably Russia and
Argentina.

The graded wheat still all goes under the name of
"Manitoban," though, at the present time, more wheat is
grown in Saskatchewan than in Manitoba. The grades
descend from the "fancy" No. 1 Hard to No. 6 Northern
Manitoba, tough, and Nos. 1, 2 and 3 Alberta Red Winter,
feed wheat; of these, the standards for the first three grades
are fixed by law, those for the others by regulation from year
to year. The inspection and grading, carried out by Government experts, take place at Winnipeg, through where practically all the wheat passes on its way to the large terminal
ports of Duluth, Buffalo, Fort William and Port Arthur.
Students should acquaint themselves with the permanent
and variable bases of Manitoban grading. These two
latter ports have unrivalled facilities for dealing rapidly
and economically with the large quantities of grain that
arrive for shipment. Each year sees extensions in the storage
and handling capacity of the ports.

13

Most of the wheat grown in Western Canada is of the Spring variety—the peculiar conditions of soil and climate are, as we have noted previously, especially suitable for the growth of a magnificent strong wheat. A little Winter wheat is grown on the southern border of Alberta and in the eastern parts of the Dominion, but only little is exported.

Northern Manitoba—the cream of which is classified as Number 1 Hard—is a red wheat, hard in structure. bright and attractive in appearance, having long, plump, well-filled, good-sized berries—larger than Spring American —of high natural weight, in good condition, and yielding a fairly high percentage of flour. The flour made from this wheat is of great strength, and produces a large, well-piled loaf of excellent colour and quite good flavour—in parenthesis, a mixture of this wheat and choice English makes the best flavoured bread in the world. The pile, flavour and texture of the loaf will be excellent, but the crust may be a little inclined to redness and toughness. As from Spring wheat, a large number of loaves per sack of flour can be obtained from Manitobas. In the mill this wheat is excellent to work and yields admirable results if well handled. Impurities few, cockle, seeds, oats, barley and buckwheat.

No. 2 Northern Manitoba is slightly lower in quality than No. 1, of a less natural weight, with not quite the same superlative strength, but is another fine milling wheat. Here and there a soft grain may be seen, while there are rather more impurities and the general appearance lacks the lustre and attractiveness which characterise the best grade.

No. 3 Northern Manitoba shows a considerable drop in value, estimated in the market by about 1/- per quarter. There is often a number of frosted grains present, which make the wheat work a little uncertainly, while the sound wheat is not of such high quality and natural weight. The grains are duller and lack the bright, clear, handsome appearance characteristic of the best grade. The flour yield will be markedly less, and the percentage of the impurities more, while the colour and strength of the flour will be somewhat impaired. This wheat, however, is a good average "strong" wheat for inserting in a mixture designed to produce a fair average flour.

No. 4 and 5 Manitobas.—These low grade wheats appeared in large quantities in England in 1912; they con sist of small shrivelled and frosted grains, with a large percentage of impurities of all kinds, while the good grains are dull and uninviting in appearance and often there is more than a suspicion of smut; they must be conditioned very carefully. The flour is of poor quality and the strength very much impaired, the colour is very dark and the flour percentages in the case of No. 4 will not be above 64, and of No. 5 anything below 60. Altogether these wheats are very unsatisfactory to use and though of low price are expensive to work.

There is a relatively small amount of soft red and white Canadian wheat grown, neither of which practically ever appears in England—their properties are similar to those of English, except that neither the colour nor the flavour is equal to that of the home-grown grain.

Such in brief are some of the main characteristics of the better known varieties of wheat at present grown in North America.

CANADA.

PRODUCTION OF WHEAT.

Harvested August.		Spring & Winter. Qrs.
1910	....	16,500,000
1911	....	28,800,000
1912	....	28,000,000
1913	....	29,000,000
1914	....	20,100,000

N.B.—Almost 90 per cent. of Canada's Crop is Spring sown.

EXPORTS BY CANADA TO ALL DESTINATIONS,

According to Official Canadian Returns.

Season ended 31st Aug.	Wheat. Qrs., 480 lbs.	Flour. Sacks, 280 lbs.	Total as Wheat. Qrs., 480 lbs.
1911	6,512,600	2,283,600	8,415,000
1912	9,866,100	2,991,400	12,358,900
1913	12,234,100	3,063,100	14,786,700
1914	13,957,800	3,266,400	16,679,800
1915	7,797,100	3,428,000	10,653,800

WHEAT AND THE FLOUR MILL.

IMPORTS OF CANADIAN WHEAT & FLOUR BY THE U.K.

Season ended 31st July.	Wheat. Qrs., 480 lbs.	Flour. Sacks, 280 lbs.	Total as Wheat. Qrs., 480 lbs.
1911	3,147,000	1,139,000	4,090,000
1912	4,486,000	1,544,000	5,772,000
1913	4,866,000	1,593,000	6,194,000
1914	5,706,000	1,628,000	7,064,000
1915	6,405,000	1,234,000	7,433,000

The above are British Board of Trade figures and are not to be absolutely relied upon owing to the peculiar manner in which they are compiled.

CANADIAN EXPORTS TO ALL DESTINATIONS,

According to Official Canadian Returns.

Season ended 31st Aug.	Wheat. Qrs., 480 lbs.	Flour. Sacks, 280 lbs.	Total as Wheat. Qrs., 480 lbs.
1911	6,512,600	2,283,600	8,415,600
1912	9,866,100	2,991,400	12,358,900
1913	12,234,100	3,063,100	14,786,700
1914	13,957,800	3,266,400	16,679,800
1915	7,797,100	3,428,000	10,653,800

CANADA.
CROP.

Harvested August.	*Wheat—Spring & Winter. Qrs.
1910	16,506,000
1911	28,865,000
1912	28,020,000
1913	28,965,000
1914	20,160,000

* About 13 per cent. is Winter.

CANADA.

*IMPORTS INTO U.K. FROM CANADIAN PORTS.

Season ended 31st July	Wheat. Qrs., 480 lbs.	Flour. Sacks, 280 lbs.	Total as Wheat. Qrs., 480 lbs.
1911	3,147,200	1,139,200	4,096,500
1912	4,486,000	1,544,300	5,772,900
1913	4,866,400	1,593,500	6,194,300
1914	5,706,900	1,628,800	7,064,200
1915	6,404,900	1,233,800	7,433,100

*These British Board of Trade returns sometimes mislead, as United States wheat and flour are exported through Canadian ports and some Canadian wheat and flour through United States ports.

South America.

The varieties of wheat grown throughout the southern half of the Continent of South America next claim our attention. As a wheat producer, South America has attained only recently to importance, but now it ranks among the largest of the World's exporters.

In only a small number of the many States of South America is wheat grown at all extensively, and from only three, viz., Uruguay, Chili and Argentina is it exported to Europe, and of these three States the first two are of very minor consequence—so that the Argentine Republic stands alone as an important and increasing wheat exporter. With this great exception it is worthy of note that the remainder of the South American States do not show any signs of materially increasing their wheat production. In particular, the exports from Chili and Uruguay, both of which were looked upon a few years ago as likely to become large shippers, have remained stationary or actually declined.

The conditions of climate and soil which make wheat production possible obtain over a very wide area in South America; the cereal is grown in all latitudes between 10 degrees North and 47 degrees South. Commercially, however, it is only cultivated between the thirtieth and forty-second parallels South latitude. As in North America, the tendency has been for the wheat region to extend towards the poles and in Argentina particularly has this been the case during the last few years.

The wheat-importing countries need not be mentioned, with the exception of Peru and Brazil. In both of these States there are wide tracts of country having conditions of soil and climate suitable for the growth of wheat. It does not, however, appear probable that in the reasonably near future these countries will become extensive wheat growers. On the other hand, they will probably remain, as now, dependent for their foodstuffs upon Argentina and Uruguay. Experts have recognised for some time that Uruguay is a country having conditions of soil and climate favourable to the cultivation of wheat. Expansion, however, has been slow, and the grain and flour exports fluctuate from year to year. Some of the wheat exported comes to Europe, but a large proportion goes to the neighbouring State of Brazil. Its characteristics are similar in most respects to average samples of Plate wheat and call for no particular comment.

Chili, which ranks second among the wheat-producing countries of South America, is one of the oldest countries now exporting wheat to England. The wheat is grown throughout a long narrow area, under greatly differing conditions of soil and climate, and this accounts in part for the rather variable qualities of the samples which arrive in this country. Wheat is cultivated alike on semi-arid and irrigated lands, but the greater part is grown in the central zone where the climate is generally warm and equable and the rainfall only moderate. A little red wheat is grown in the Northern region, but the bulk of the crop is white. Chilian white wheat is a dry wheat varying in structure between mild to hard. The berries are of medium size, with a very thin, brittle skin. Before washing became general, complaint was made that the wheat yielded " blue " flour, but with careful conditioning a fairly high yield of dead-white flour can be obtained. The strength is low, but the yield and dead-white colour make Chilian a very useful wheat to add to the mixture, especially when other wheats which break down yellow are included.

Impurities are usually present in considerable proportions and consist chiefly of seeds, stones, barley and dirt

In the North, the wheat is sown during May and June and harvested in December; in the South, it is sown a month later and reaping lasts from February to April, the principal crop being harvested in February. During the past two seasons the U.K. has received only about 50,000 quarters, whereas in the three preceding seasons we received between 300,000 and 400,000 quarters per annum. Peru also usually claims about 100,000 quarters of Chili's wheat.

Argentine Wheats.

We now come to the consideration of the one great wheat-producing State of South America—the Argentine Republic. Of recent years the growth and development of the agricultural resources of Argentina have been surpassed by no country and equalled—and then only in the matter of grain raising—by Canada alone. It is true that of the natural resource of the country there never has been a doubt, even so, the manner in which resources, railways, wheat lands, corn fields, cattle raising simultaneously have been developed can only be described as phenomenal. The history of the expansion—from the Paraguayan War, of 1865, to the financial crisis of 1891, and from that time until the present day—makes a very fascinating study and one worth pursuing for its own sake, but it cannot be dwelt upon here.

Wheat is grown in Argentina over an area extending from latitude 30 South to 40 South and even further South there are small districts, such as Chubut, where the cereal is also cultivated, though on quite a small scale. Westward from Buenos Aires, the wheat area extends for about 400 miles, thus making the great oblong 400 miles by 800 miles, upon which the premier cereal can be profitably produced, an extent of country almost equal to three times the area of the British Isles. Over such a large tract of country, there are, of course, considerable differences of climate, but, speaking generally, between the 30th and 40th parallels there is a climate with plenty of sunshine and usually an adequate rainfall favourable for the production of wheat. The rainfall in the South is light and irregular and severe droughts from time to time do great damage. The wheat is chiefly grown on the wide, undulating " Pampas," or plains, with neither tree nor hill visible for hundreds of miles. The soil on these Pampas almost everywhere is rich, and usually consists of alluvial deposit containing a considerable amount of vegetable matter, and distinctly favourable for wheat growing. In the tracts near the great river, the black earth is many feet deep, but westward its depth decreases until it is a mere covering of a few inches upon the light sand of the desert. The Argentine wheat regions may be divided into three main divisions :—

1. The Durum district of the extreme North.
2. The central zone, which grows the wheat that is despatched from the river ports.
3. The Southern and Western districts, which ship wheat largely from Bahia Blanca.

These divisions are, of course, only general and are merely adopted for convenience.

The system of selling Argentine wheat has often been unsatisfactory and has given rise to considerable friction. Probably it is also partly responsible for the reputation of unreliability which attaches to Plate wheat. Cargoes are sold on natural weight basis with allowances for deficiencies in weight at the port of arrival, but the system has not worked altogether well and often operates to the detriment of the buyer.

Mention has been made of the mildness of the climate, which allows the land to be worked throughout the year; the system of farming practised calls for some little remark. The greater number of the agricultural settlers in the Argentine are Italian peasants. The land is farmed by family labour, the system of farming is poor and uneconomical, the farmers are men of no substance and have no capital to enable them to farm on a scientific basis; mixed and rotatory farming is nearly unknown—while any land showing signs of devitalisation is passed over and abandoned. This is an easy matter on the treeless plains and is in marked contrast with the clearing operations that have to be done in some parts of Canada. On the other hand, the soil of the Pampas is not equal to that of the prairies, while the Canadian farmer has no fear of locusts. These insects have done great damage to crops in time past and their power for evil is not yet broken, but the methods adopted by the Government for their destruction have been carefully organised throughout the country. Argentine farmers live in hope that, in the course of time. these pests will be exterminated, as they have been in other parts of the world, but their final extinction will not be for many scores of years. The Argentine farmer, unlike the Canadian, does not own his land; he is a tenant, often on a kind of profit-sharing system, and this does not tend to produce a better system of farming.

Argentine wheats shipped to this country are practically all of the red type. Barletta—originally imported from Italy —is the favourite variety and is grown throughout the country, but, principally in the North. Russian and Hungarian varieties of seed wheat were imported and have given their names to certain commercial grades. The commonest commercial grades are Rosafe, Barusso and Baril. It should be noted that, with the exception of Rosafe and Barusso, the grade names are not very reliable, while the lower grades of Plate wheat all tend to merge into a common type.

Rosafe wheat is a red wheat, thin in berry, small and of medium hardness, with a characteristic red tinge, especially noticeable in the better varieties. The yield of flour is high from good samples. The flour is very white—the patents are almost the whitest in the world, and Plate wheats are easily the best for colour among foreign reds. They are of medium strength, and millers usually reckon that these wheats will rather more than "carry themselves" in a mixture. The flavour is sweet, but Plates tend to produce a crust red and rough, or as it is termed "foxy." They work well in the mill and dry samples take a moderate amount of water very quickly. Care must be taken with conditioning in order to correct a tendency in the flour to dress a little bare towards the tail of the system.

Barusso is another variety which is exported in considerable quantities. It derives its name from a part of each of the names of the seed wheats from which it was originally grown—Barletta and Russian. It is a red wheat grown in the South and West and mostly shipped from Bahia Blanca. It is hard in structure, is rather plumper than Rosafe. The qualities are very similar; there is, however, not quite the same brilliance in the flour, the yield is perhaps a little higher. Altogether Barusso is an excellent milling wheat.

WHEAT AND THE FLOUR MILL.

Summing up it may be said that Plate wheats in general are extremely useful to the miller and are very popular, being usually obtainable at a reasonable price and being also able to "take care of themselves" in a mixture, while they work well in the mill, and help to produce a flour liked by bakers.

Impurities exist in all Plate wheats in considerable quantities; in the lower grades there is often a great cleaning loss. They consist mainly of screenings, chaff, oats, barley and dirt.

The wheat is sown in April and May, and harvested in late November-December.

There remains to be considered the "yellow" Durum wheats of the extreme North. These wheats are hard, thin-skinned, uncertain in working and rather coarse.

The chief varieties of Durum are Saldome and Candeal, being grown in the extreme North of the country. The crop is but small, however, and is wholly consumed by local macaroni manufacturers and semolina mills. The properties are similar to those of other Durum wheats and need not be given in detail here.

The above concludes the list of better-known South American wheats, those only have been treated in any detail which come within the ken of English millers.

ARGENTINA.
Production of Wheat.
Official Estimate.

Harvested December.		Crop. Qrs., 480 lbs.
1910	....	18,200,000
1911	....	21,400,000
1912	....	*24,800,000
1913	....	14,200,000
1914	....	21,400,000

*Believed to have been overestimated by 4,000,000 qrs.

Exports by Argentina to All Destinations,
According to Argentine Official Returns.

Calendar year.		Wheat & Flour as Wheat. Qrs., 480 lbs.
1911	....	11,288,000
1912	....	12,957,000
1913	....	13,751,000
1914	....	4,951,000
1915	....	12,314,000

IMPORTS OF ARGENTINE WHEAT & FLOUR BY U.K.

Season ended 31st July.	Wheat. Qrs., 480 lbs.	Flour. Sacks, 280 lbs.
1911	4,044,000	61,000
1912	3,642,000	22,000
1913	4,723,000	80,100
1914	1,782,000	47,400
1915	2,817,000	8,300

ARGENTINA.

CROP & EXPORTS.—WHEAT.

Official Argentine Return.

Harvested December.	Crop. Qrs., 480 lbs.	•Calendar Year.	Subsequent Exports. Wheat & Flour as Wheat Qrs., 480 lbs.
1910	18,200,000	1911	11,288,400
1911	21,400,000	1912	12,956,700
1912	*24,800,000	1913	13,751,100
1913	14,200,000	1914	4,951,700
1914	21,400,000	1915	12,314,500

* Commercial estimate 21,000,000 quarters.

ARGENTINA.

IMPORTS INTO U.K.

Season ended 31st July.	Wheat. Qrs., 480 lbs.	Flour. Sacks, 280 lbs.
1911	4,044,100	61,100
1912	3,642,200	22,400
1913	4,722,900	80,100
1914	1,781,600	47,400
1915	2,817,500	8,300

Asia and Australasia.

As a wheat producer Asia does not figure as largely as its vast extent, and teeming population, would seem to warrant. India is the only important exporting country and even in that case the quantity of wheat shipped does not amount to more than about 15 per cent. of the total crop. The consumption of Wheat is, however, increasing in several eastern countries—notably in China, Japan and Manchuria. In each of these countries roller mills have been erected, moreover the imports of flour from the Pacific Coast of America are becoming quite substantial. To what extent the consumption of bread will reach in the East it is impossible to say, but it would appear that from the nature of the conditions under which the people live, and from the fact that wheat is more costly to raise than is rice, that the latter must remain the staple food of the eastern races, at any rate for a very long time.

Four Asiatic countries only export wheat and of these four, the exports from three are of a negligible quantity. The four countries (in reverse order of importance) are Manchuria, Turkey-in-Asia, Persia and India. Taking the unimportant countries first, Manchuria grows a fair quantity of red wheat which has occasionally been seen in England and, if cheap, it might be found a useful wheat, but of no great strength. From Turkey in Asia occasionally comes a parcel of hard, rather rough-looking white or mixed wheat. It is usually dirty and is not a good milling wheat. Persia has again become an exporter of wheat to this country. The wheat is a dirty white colour, very hard in structure and needs very thorough washing and conditioning. Its strength is low and the milling qualities are only moderate. Altogether it is not a good milling wheat and can only be used in mixtures not designed to produce the highest class of flour. There are usually a large number of impurities consisting of barley (often in large quantities), stones, dirt, etc.

Although Persia is shipping rather more freely than formerly, the aggregate importance of all the above wheats is but small and this account of them is inserted here mainly for the benefit of the student and as a matter of record.

India.

During the last few years the exports of wheat from our Indian Empire have increased considerably and for the past four seasons India has been high on the list of countries exporting wheat to the United Kingdom. The export surplus, however, amounts only to a relatively small proportion of the total crop, generally about 10 to 15 per cent. after a very good harvest, as from that of the year 1912.

There are three main wheat-growing regions in India :

1. The Punjaub and Sind—export port, Kurrachee

2. The United Provinces—export ports, Kurrachee, Calcutta and Bombay.

3. Sind and part of the Central Provinces—the ports of which are principally Kurrachee and Bombay

Of these by far the most important, at any rate from the English point of view, is the Punjaub district on account of the fact that it produces a much larger surplus for export than any other district. Of the big wheat-exporting countries India has about the hottest climate and every year the wheat crop largely depends upon the monsoon. Irrigation, however, is being greatly increased and the wheat crop is becoming less and less dependent upon the rainfall. Over an area as wide as that in which wheat is cultivated in India there are, of course, many varieties of soil. How wide the wheat area of India is may be described in the words of a recent writer : " From the numerous mouths of the Ganges there extends a vast alluvial plain which is only lost in the North-west Provinces and the Punjaub by blending into the drainage area of the Indus and may be said to widen until it reaches the Northern division of Bombay." Throughout the whole of this region wheat is cultivated in varying degrees of intensity.

In the Central Provinces and Berar the wheat is grown on the " black cotton soil." This is of great richness, and has a large water absorbing, and consequently drought resist ing, capacity. In the Bombay Presidency there are many soils ranging in character from very rich to sandy and poor; in the other regions the soil is of an alluvial character.

The methods of farming by the ryot (native farmer) are crude in the extreme, but by a modified system of rotatory farming and the custom of sowing mixed and leguminous crops, he avoids the danger of exhausting his land.

In most districts his implements, however, are of the rudest character, the pattern of plough is often archaic, and the patriarchal system of threshing the corn by treading it out on a mud floor by oxen is still in vogue. The storage facilities for wheat are extremely poor and there are in India but very few of the elevators and none of the elaborate grain-handling systems that are found in Canada or the United States or even in Argentina. The amount of refuse and rubbish and extraneous matter that is often present in Indian wheat was for a long time a sore point with millers, but since the introduction of the new contract there is very little to complain of in this respect.

Of all the Indian grades of wheat which arrive in this country, Choice White Kurrachee is by far the most abundant and consequently the most important of all Indian grades. Nominally a white wheat, there is usually some admixture of red. It is a medium-sized grain, hard in structure and of a somewhat dull appearance. In the uncleaned sample there is present, as in all Indian wheats, a pungent odour liable to communicate itself to the flour if the conditioning process be not carefully carried out. Kurrachee is of medium strength and gives a good yield of flour which, however, is apt to make the texture of the loaf coarse. It breaks down yellow and has done much to extend the use of bleaching in this country. The flavour is inclined to be strong and dry, but careful conditioning will eliminate the harsh flavour, though it will be insipid to the last. The wheat needs very careful and thorough washing and if that be given much of the natural harshness and pungency can be eliminated. Kurrachee takes up a large amount of water, but does so slowly and two washings and even steaming are needed. Kurrachee on account of its great water-absorbing capacity—a characteristic shared by other Indian varieties—and the fact that it usually cheapens the mixture is much liked by millers in this country and as a wheat not liable to vary—and to fill up a mixture or to act as a set-off against damp or out-of-condition wheats it is very valuable. The fact, too, that even after conditioning it imparts a good water-absorbing capacity to the flour makes it a good wheat to introduce into mixtures designed to produce flour to be used by bakers.

Red Kurrachee arrives in fair quantities in this country. it is dry red wheat of medium strength, which breaks down very yellow and has a harsh taste which must be corrected by long and thorough conditioning. It is a useful and reliable wheat to add to a mixture.

From Calcutta in some years comes a fair quantity of wheat, but nothing to compare with the amount that is shipped from Kurrachee.

White No. 1 Club Calcutta is a fine white wheat giving a good yield of superior quality flour and it is about the strongest of foreign whites. No. 2 Club Calcutta is another very useful wheat considerably stronger than Kurrachee—it is a very good wheat to add to a mixture. It breaks down a trifle yellow, but not so yellow as Kurrachee.

Choice White Bombay is a fine wheat which bulks well. In structure it is very dry and hard, but not so hard as Calcutta. It is an excellent " colour " wheat and, properly conditioned, yields well. The strength is rather lower than that of Calcutta wheats.

In the Delhi district both red and white wheats are grown and White Delhi is a wheat giving an excellent yield of high-coloured flour, which will give a better texture and flavour to the loaf than any other Indian wheat. Its strength, however, is only low. Red Delhi is stronger than White Delhi, but the loaf made therefrom has not such a good flavour or texture. It much resembles Hard White Calcutta. in general characteristics.

All Indian wheats contain more or less impurities. These vary in amount from 1 to 5 per cent. and consist of earth, stones, barley, gram, etc., but for a few years past nearly all Indian wheats have been bought on the basis of " clean terms," which limit the proportion of non-farinaceous matter to 2 per cent. Formerly the proportion of impurities often amounted to as much as 10 to 12 per cent.

Such is a brief description of Indian wheats.

WHEAT AND THE FLOUR MILL.

INDIA.

PRODUCTION OF WHEAT.

Harvested March/April.		Wheat Crop. Qrs., 480 lbs.
1910	....	46,716,000
1911	....	45,800,000
1912	....	46,645,000
1913	....	45,110,000
1914	....	38,410,000

EXPORTS BY INDIA TO ALL DESTINATIONS.

Season ended 31st March.		Wheat & Flour. Qrs., 480 lbs.
1911	....	5,909,000
1912	....	6,357,000
1913	....	7,747,000
1914	....	5,610,000
1915	....	3,312,000

IMPORTS OF INDIAN WHEAT & FLOUR BY THE U.K.,

According to British Board of Trade Figures.

Season ended 31st July.		Qrs., 480 lbs.
1911	....	5,045,000
1912	....	4,673,000
1913	....	5,675,000
1914	....	2,964,000
1915	....	3,254,000

Only a small percentage of India's Wheat reaches the U.K. in a manufactured state.

INDIA.

WHEAT CROP AND TOTAL EXPORTS.

Harvested in April.	Crop Harvested in April. Qrs., 480 lbs.	Season ended 31st March.	Exports to all Destinations. Qrs., 480 lbs.
1910	46,716,000	1911	5,908,704
1911	45,796,000	1912	6,357,289
1912	46,645,000	1913	7,474,540
1913	45,109,000	1914	5,610,290
1914	38,409,000	1915	3,312,000

INDIA.

IMPORTS INTO U.K.

Season ended 31st July.		Wheat. Qrs.
1911	....	5,045,200
1912	....	4,673,200
1913	....	5,675,300
1914	....	2,964,200
1915	....	3,253,900

Australasia

From Australia there is imported annually a considerable quantity of wheat that is much liked by millers. The quantity has increased fairly steadily during recent years and the proportion of exports to production is high. The conditions of agriculture and climate do not call for any extended comment. Wheat is principally grown in the west of the ten-inch rainfall line in Victoria, New South Wales and South Australia. The soil is generally light and sandy; the climate is hot and dry, and the rainfall, when it comes, is often heavy, but unfortunately it is not at all regular and from time to time droughts do great damage to the crops. This lack of rainfall constitutes the chief handicap under which the Australian farmers labour.

Australian wheat usually seen on our markets is white or rather straw tinted, dry but mellow in structure, with a large handsome regular berry, very pleasing to the eye. The yield of flour is very high indeed—the highest of all foreign wheats. The flour is of a beautifully pale golden tinted colour, with an excellent bloom, and the berry breaks down easily under the rolls. Its strength is fair only. Australian takes water very quickly, being only rivalled in this respect by the drier Pacific sorts, and this propensity must be taken into account when washing the wheat, otherwise it may become water-logged. The impurities are very few. Australians are much liked by millers on account of their high colour and yielding properties and the bloom they impart to the flour and are of great value in a mixture designed to produce a long length of good patents.

New Zealand sometimes sends a few cargoes of wheat to this country, but in recent years their number has greatly decreased. The conditions of soil and climate are not unlike those that obtain in the British Isles. The wheats, which are about equal to second quality English, are of two kinds (a) long berried, of a yellow colour, and mild in structure, and (b) short berried, both white and red, which is a small soft kind. The yield and colour of flour from all varieties is quite good and they are fairly clean. They are, however, very soft and amongst the weakest wheats in the world.

AUSTRALIA.

PRODUCTION OF WHEAT.

Harvested December.		Wheat Crop. Qrs., 480 lbs.
1910	....	11,890,000
1911	....	8,958,000
1912	....	11,136,000
1913	....	12,986,000
1914	....	3,331,000

Calendar Year.	Exports by Australia to all Destinations According to Official Australian Returns. Qrs., 480 lbs.	Season ended 31st July.	Imports of Australian Wheat & Flour by the U.K., According to British Board of Trade Figures. Qrs. 480 lbs.
1911	7,928,000	1911	2,523,000
1912	5,079,000	1912	3,723,000
1913	6,328,000	1913	2,633,000
1914	7,646,000	1914	3,630,000
1915	175,000	1915	463,000

N.B.—Only a small percentage of Australia's Wheat reaches the U.K. in a manufactured state.

AUSTRALIA.

WHEAT AND FLOUR TOGETHER.

Year ended 31st December.	Total Years' Exports by Commonwealth. Qrs., 480 lbs.	Season ended 31st July.	Quantity Imported by U.K. from Commonwealth. Qrs., 480 lbs.
1911	7,928,100	1911	2,523,400
1912	5,079,500	1912	3,723,100
1913	6,324,000	1913	2,633,800
1914	7,646,800	1914	3,630,200
1915	175,400	1915	463,100

AUSTRALIA.

CROP.—WHEAT.

December. Harvested		Qrs. Wheat.
1910	....	11,889,000
1911	....	8,958,000
1912	....	11,136,000
1913	....	12,986,000
1914	....	3,331,000

Africa

Africa from the point of view of the English miller is of no importance as a wheat producer whatever. A little wheat, but only a little, is grown in the South, but not sufficient for home consumption. Egypt occasionally sents a parcel of very inferior wheat which is almost worthless from a milling point of view. It is white or mixed, coarse, harsh, dry and poor in colour and flavour, and absolutely weak. Practically none now arrives in this country.

Algerian and Tunisian wheat formerly was exported to this country in moderate quantities, but France now is the only importer from these countries.

Europe is the continent of " consumption." Nearly the whole of the surplus of the other continents comes to Europe, and so, although the various European countries, with hardly any exception, grow considerable crops, their wheats do not directly affect the British miller as with the exceptions noted below they are never exported to these islands. The exceptions to this rule are the wheats of Russia and the Danubian States. For many years Russia has been the largest European exporter. The Danubian or Balkan States —Roumania, Bulgaria and Servia, also export in the aggre gate a substantial quantity of wheat.

Russia.

Russia, which has for many years been one of the World's chief wheat exporters, is the land to which millers may look for wheat when at any time North American strong wheats are for any reason unavailable. Although Russian wheat is always considered a European wheat, not all of it is grown on this side of the Urals; indeed, the potentialities of Russia in Asia may be said to be perhaps greater than those of Russia in Europe, for there are still tens of millions of acres in Siberia well adapted for wheat growing, waiting to be brought under cultivation. It has already been noted that Russia is the producer and probably the original producer of really strong wheats. In the Southern States the soil on

which these are grown is very rich, and the yield per acre is
relatively high, but on the vast Steppes—high tablelands
corresponding in many respects to the prairies and pampas of
North and South America, the fertility of the soil is much
less and the average yield per acre in fairly good crop years
is not more than ten bushels, but the extent of the area
ensures a great crop in the aggregate. The average yield of
Winter wheat is fourteen bushels per acre and that of Spring
wheat is nine bushels. The conditions of soil and climate
resemble somewhat those obtaining in the Canadian strong
wheat lands. The climate in the winter is very severe and
there is almost always a heavy snowfall; the spring, as known
in this country, lasts for a few days only and the summer
comes very suddenly and is hot with brilliant sunshine during the ripening and harvest months, but in recent years the
rainfall at harvest time has been abnormally heavy as in
Canada recently. The methods of farming are crude and
there is always present in the wheat a considerable quantity
of impurities, principally in the form of weed seeds, barley
and rye. In the U.K. Russian wheat is almost invariably
bought on sample, the old commercial type names having
fallen into disuse; but on the Continent Russian wheat is
now very largely bought with a guarantee of its natural
weight and with an allowance for impurities. The two
principal kinds of Russian wheat are Azima, meaning
Winter, and Ghirka under which all the Spring-sown varieties are usually classed. During the last five years the
Russian crop has consisted of the following proportions of
Winter and Spring wheat :—

RUSSIAN WHEAT CROP.

	Winter—Qrs.	Spring—Qrs.	Total—Qrs.
1908	18.400,000	52,500,000	70,900 000
1909	25,800,000	71,800,000	97,600,000
1910	34,800,000	69,300,000	104,100,000
1911	23,026,000	39,000,000	62.026,000
1912	29,699,000	60,100,000	89,799.000
1913	34.020,300	82,280,000	116,501,200
1914	26,593,000	66,924,900	93,517,000

During the same time Russia's exports to all destinations have been as follows :—

SEASON ENDED 31ST JULY.

	Qrs.
1907 08	7,592,000
1908-09	12,076,000
1909-10	27,849,000
1910-11	27,972,000
1911-12	9,946,000
1912-13	12,461,500
1913-14	20,740,800

The U.K. in those five seasons imported the following quantities of Russian wheat :—

IMPORTS INTO U.K. OF RUSSIAN WHEAT.

Season ended 31st July.

	Qrs.
1907-08	1,236,000
1908-09	2,025,000
1909-10	6,101,000
1910-11	6,285,000
1911-12	2,199,000
1912-13	1,782,300
1913-14	2,274,700

South Russian is a generally smallish red wheat, long and thin in the berry and of medium hardness. Each season there are many samples of greatly differing qualities, but a good average sample weighs well and gives an average yield of flour which is of full strength. It is for their strength that Russian varieties are included among the wheats of the first class. The colour of a loaf made from Russian flour will be quite fair, its texture will be rather coarse, and the crust tends to be a little red. In the mill the flour is inclined to dress a little grey towards the tail of the system, and care must always be taken with the conditioning—the wheat absorbs water rather slowly. This, of course, applies to sound heavy wheat. Usually Russians contain a fair proportion of light grains which soak up water at first contact. The bloom produced in the loaf will not be so good as that in loaves made from the best strong American flours, with the exception of the finest Azimas.

D

WHEAT AND THE FLOUR MILL.

The wheat shipped from North Russian ports is the produce, as a rule, of Siberia, but a certain proportion comes from Poland and the region of the West-central provinces, this wheat resembles the afore-mentioned in most respects, but does not arrive in this country in great quantities; Germany, Holland, Sweden and Denmark, owing to their proximity to North Russia, secure 80 to 90 per cent. of these supplies. The samples do not vary in quality so much as the Southern wheat, while it is a little cleaner, and is said to be a little stronger, especially that portion which comes from Siberia.

Both the above varieties make good substitutes for the North American strong wheats; poor samples, however, need very careful handling and give great trouble in the mill, though the lower grades do not lose their strength to the same extent as the low grade of North American Spring wheat.

The district known as the Crimea produces a wheat considerably above the average of any other Russian wheats. In good seasons it is a finer, bolder berried wheat, thin skinned, and for the most part unusually strong, and is almost entirely free from the impurities usually associated with South Russian wheats, and is generally offered on our market as Eupatorian.

North Russia also ships a remarkably fine and bold thin-skinned wheat in considerable quantities to the North-east ports—many millers in the Hull district use it freely when available, and in some cases have paid as much for it as No. 1 Manitobas. Some millers never quite appreciate their value, as they make a flour which appears to be of an unsatisfactory quality when baked either alone or with a normal mixing, but when blended with the right kinds improves the loaf.

Speaking of Russian wheats, as a whole, they may be said to be very valuable to millers and especially to those who possess very complete cleaning and milling systems. They need care in their use, but their strength properties make them of value, and the skilful miller can get from them excellent results.

There is usually a considerable loss in cleaning Russian wheats, and a complete cylinder equipment is required adequately to deal with the small seeds, and sometimes the rye found in them. The impurities are cockle, wild buckwheat, wild rape, rye, barley, dirt and stones. The three first-named impurities reduce the value of the wheat much more than their proportionate weight, owing to their low value when extracted.

Saxonska is a choice Russian variety of great strength and fine milling qualities. It is very seldom seen in this country now, but was formerly imported here from the Northern ports. Ulka is a new variety exported in large quantities from the South. It is a red wheat of medium strength, which works rather uncertainly in the mixture.

Kubanka is one of the Durums, but differs from the rest in being quite a strong wheat. Of flint-like hardness, it is difficult to mill, even after thorough conditioning, and gives a low yield of yellow-tinted flour which, however, makes a big loaf.

The Durum or Macaroni wheats need mention. They are grown in South-Eastern Russia, and are exported chiefly to Italy and France. They are now grown extensively in the United States.

Durums are yellow in colour, with a long, transparent grain of flinty hardness. They are exceptionally difficult to mill, and the most drastic conditioning, carried out over a period of time is needed to make them reducible. Their strength is fair to low, the colour is moderate and the flavour dry and ricey, while the yield is not high. The wheats are usually fairly clean and would increase in popularity as bread wheats if they were not kept relatively dear in the market by the demand from macaroni millers of Italy and the South of France.

Balkan States.

In the Danube basin there is a good quantity of wheat grown annually, of which a considerable percentage is exported. Generally, relatively cheap, it is well liked by millers, especially by the Belgians and Germans.

Exports of the Balkan States during the past five seasons to all countries were as follows :—

Season ended 31st July.	WHEAT. Qrs.
1907-08	2,867,000
1908-09	4,865,000
1909-10	4,891,000
1910-11	10,899,000
1911-12	9,596,000
1912-13	6,732,000
1913-14	7,634,000

The imports to the U.K. during the past five seasons were only small :—

U.K. IMPORTS FROM ROUMANIA, BULGARIA AND SERVIA.

Season ended 31st July.	WHEAT. Qrs.
1907-08	245,000
1908-09	341,000
1909-10	117,000
1910-11	320,000
1911-12	624.000
1912-13	6,860
1913-14	133,723

The wheat is red, hard in structure, with fair-sized berries, having a bright appearance. The yield of flour is good and the latter is of medium strength and fair colour, giving a nice flavour and texture to the loaf. Danubian wheats require efficient and thorough conditioning before the best results can be obtained from them. The wheats grown on the north bank of the Danube are superior to those grown on the south. They work quite well in the mill and are distinctly useful to the miller. Their quality seems steadily to improve, and impurities are not present now in such large proportions as formerly.

The wheats of the other European States practically never appear in the United Kingdom. The wheats of

Western Europe usually resemble the English type. French wheat is thick-skinned, tough, starchy; German is rather better; indeed, the old-fashioned Konigsberg and Dantzig wheats used, in former years, to be reckoned the best substitutes for English. During the past year or two Germany increased her exports of native wheat, helped by peculiar Custom House regulations; she exported nearly 2,000,000 quarters in 1912-13, of which 75,000 quarters reached this country, and was of a high quality, equal to the very best English reds. Holland, Belgium and Scandinavia are the principal importers from Germany.

Hungary cannot be passed over, though its wheat never comes to England now. It is safe to say that it is one of the very best milling wheats. The seed, the climate—severe in the winter and hot in the summer—the soil, the sufficiency and regularity of the rainfall, all combine to produce a wheat that is at once strong, of choice colour, and giving a high yield of flour that produces a loaf of good texture and sweet flavour. The best varieties are those named Theis, Banat and Bacsha, the natural weight of these wheats often reaching as high as 66 to 67 lbs. per imperial bushel.

English Wheat.

There remain to be considered the varieties of wheat grown in the United Kingdom. Home-grown wheat is no longer the predominant variety in the miller's average mixture, and not for a long time has the English harvest determined the price of the nation's bread supply, nevertheless English wheat is still valuable to millers. The many millers, too, whose mills are situated in the country or near a large wheat district, and who constitute a considerable proportion of the trade, depend on a good supply of English wheat to complete their grists.

The importance and value of English wheat as a milling variety is occasionally overlooked, especially by students and young operatives whose experience has been gained in mills where little of it is used. It is well to remember that in several respects English wheat is a valuable variety for blending with other kinds. For example, native wheat has a sweeter flavour than any other variety. Good samples also give high yields of flour of a very admirable colour. On the other hand, of course, it is impossible to use them in large proportions in merchant mill mixtures, owing to their general weakness. This great defect of native wheat is added to by the fact that nearly every year there is a quantity of wheat harvested in an unsatisfactory condition.

But it is the lack of strength which chiefly hinders a free use of English wheat. The English taste for light bread compels bakers to produce a large, well-piled loaf, which cannot be made unless the flour is fairly strong. Accordingly, millers have to supply a flour that first of all must be of good strength, otherwise it will be useful only for mixing purposes or biscuit making. This precludes the use of English wheat in very large proportions, except for the retail trade, or for special purposes. The public taste is a little difficult to explain considering that fifty years ago two-thirds of the wheat consumed annually in England was of home growth. It must be remembered, however, that the change in the taste of the public synchronised with changes in milling processes and in the character of the wheats used, as well as with the coming of American flour. Moreover, the few comparatively strong varieties of native wheat, e.g., Nursery and Red Lammas are not popular among farmers, who prefer a heavier yielding variety with weather resisting powers, e.g., Square Head's Master, or Red Chaff White. This weakness of English wheat must be taken into account when any schemes for increasing the wheat production of England are brought forward. It must not be forgotten that more than a certain quantity of English wheat of the present average strength and condition would only act as a drag upon the home market and leave the farmer in a worse plight than he was in before.

In order that something might be done to improve the quality of English wheat, the Home-Grown Wheat Committee of the National Association of British and Irish Millers was brought into existence. The Committee has now been in existence for a decade and its members have laboured arduously at the task of improving the milling qualities, and particularly the strength, of native wheat. They experimented with a number of Fife varieties imported from Canada, and found that these sorts kept their strength, when grown under English conditions, better than any other foreign strong wheats. By crossing the Fife wheats with native sorts, and by careful selection, they have succeeded in bringing out a number of new varieties. Of these the best milling sort is a hybrid known as Burgoyne's Fife—a cross between Essex Royal Chaff and one of the fixed Fifes. This is a white wheat of excellent milling quality. Good samples combine most of the qualities found in an average English wheat mixture, and milled alone they yield a good percentage of flour, strong enough to make a loaf of ordinary height and volume, having an even texture and sweet flavour. This variety, when at its best and in good condition, is undoubtedly a very fine sort and is probably the best of all English wheats for milling purposes. Of late, however, a type known as Yeoman has become first favourite and is well spoken of, especially by inland millers. The other Fife wheats grown in England also keep to a large degree their inherent characteristic of strength and consequently are liked by millers. These new, strong wheats, however, have not yet become very popular with farmers, who complain that they can get but little more money for them than for the ordinary varieties and consequently they prefer to grow the older, " safer " sorts with which they have been always familiar. Whether or not the Fife and other new strong varieties that may be introduced will become popular " farmers' " wheats, time only will show.

Speaking generally, assuming a standard sample in good condition, English wheat, in many respects, is a very useful wheat to add to the mixture. Its colour is excellent, the bloom given to the flour by the best white sort is hard to equal, while both red and white sorts produce the best flavoured bread of all the world's wheats. Its use in limited proportions improves the texture of the loaf, and serves as an admirable corrective to wheats such as Kurrachee or Manitoba, which tend to give a coarse texture to the loaf. The yield of flour obtainable varies according to the kind and the quality of the sample milled, but from well-developed, dry wheat a very high percentage of flour is obtainable. The high moisture content of home-grown grain makes it rather difficult to mill, and a great amount of skill is required to bring damp English wheat into milling condition. The subject of conditioning English wheat, however, is too large a one to enter upon at this point.

As a rule, English wheat is very clean; in fact, it is the cleanest of all wheats, the impurities consisting only of a little chaff and a few seeds. Smut is sometimes present. Garlic also is present as an admixture in certain districts. In wet seasons the miller has to beware of samples containing sprouted grains, or incipiently sprouted grains, as these, if numerous, destroy the baking properties of the flour and render the bread sodden.

A list of the principal English varieties is given below, together with very brief notes. The Fife varieties mentioned above are not included.

CLASS I.

Nursery (old fashioned) a long-berried, small, red wheat—not unlike good Plate—long considered one of the strongest and best of English milling wheats, when sown in the autumn.

Nursery (improved or Biddle's) has a rounder, plumper corn and gives a better yield per acre than the above, but is not equal to it in milling qualities.

Red Lammas is a long-berried, large wheat of good comparative strength and fine colour—by some millers preferred to Nursery. Has a long straw and is liable to fall down during rough weather.

Talavera is a white and fine comparatively strong milling wheat giving a high flour yield, but it is not a prolific sort.

Rough Chaff (White) : This is an excellent wheat, fairly strong (for English) and yields flour well. It has short straw and a square, thick-set ear and is prolific on good ground, but is rather liable to weather damage.

Rough Chaff (Essex) is a similar wheat, but with larger ears and straw, and is one of the best English wheats.

Chidham (White) is a fine old-fashioned wheat giving a high yield of good quality flour. It is not extensively grown and is not prolific.

Trump and Normandy White come in this class, but they have not been largely grown of late years.

CLASS II.

Webb's Challenge is a white wheat and one of the best of the newer varieties for milling. It gives a long length of good-flavoured flour of fair strength and might almost be included in class one.

Square Head (Red) is so called because the "set" of berries to the ear is square chested. It is a prolific variety under good conditions, but is subject to blight. It produces a weak flour and thick bran.

Square Head's Master (Teverson's) is a stronger, better selection of Square Head—but is also subject to blight. It is kept out of the first class by its lack of strength.

White Queen is a favourite farmers' variety, being a heavy yielder, but it is very susceptible to weather damage. It is thin-skinned and yields a high percentage of very excellent coloured flour.

Red Chaff (White) is a hybrid and is very prolific having, in slightly lesser degree, about the same milling qualities as White Queen.

"Golden Drop" is a well-known variety, it is thick-skinned, yields well and is hardy, but is not a very reliable milling wheat and sometimes works "soapy" in the mill.

CLASS III.

Rivetts.—This class of wheat has very long awns, which are very sharp and protect the grain from birds. It is very prolific—over 100 grains have been counted in a single ear— but the straw is poor and the chaff is useless. Rivetts produce a very weak flour of moderate colour, but of very sweet flavour. The bran is thick and the percentage of flour low—the flour is excellent for biscuit making. The French varieties, grown of late years in this country, give generally fairly good yields of wheat per acre, but their milling qualities, as a rule, are somewhat defective. The best known are Marvel Perfection, Gros, Eclipse and Hatif Invincible.

The characteristics of the wheats mentioned in the above list must be taken as being occasionally liable to vary. Indeed the properties of several English varieties vary considerably according to the local conditions under which they are grown.

A SUGGESTIVE STATEMENT, COPIED FROM THE CORN TRADE YEAR BOOK.

By G. J. S. BROOMHALL, F.S.S.

DECADES	AVAILABLE FOR CONSUMPTION			Percentage of British Produce to Total Supply	Population (Middle of Harvest Year)	Average Gazette Price per Quarter Cereal Year
	Home Produce, less 2¼ bus. per acre for seed	Imports, less Exports—Wheat and Flour	TOTAL Native and Foreign			
	Qrs.	Qrs.	Qrs.			s. d.
1852-53—1861-62......	12,641,006	5,633,570	18,274,576	69·1	28,257,451	57 5
1862-63—1871-72......	12,825,581	8,062,493	20,888,074	61·4	30,314,885	5
1872-73—1881-82......	9,378,225	13,961,194	23,339,419	41·8	33,543, 76	49 4
1882-83—1891-92......	8,7 8,029	18,686,202	27,434,231	31·9	36,777,398	34 0
1892-93—1901-02......	6,668,400	22,811,600	29,479,700	22·5	40,053,900	27 4
1902-03—1911-12......	6,525,300	26,228,500	32,753,800	19·9	43,930,300	30 6

* Cost of the whole supply reckoned at the Gazette price of Native wheat.

THE STORAGE AND HANDLING OF WHEAT.

THE INTAKE PLANT.

SILOS AND PRELIMINARY CLEANING PLANT.

The initial operation in the business of flour milling is the purchase of wheat by the miller. After he has bought his wheat he has to get it into his mill, then he has to store it for a greater or less time. At each of these stages it is perfectly easy—through lack of skill in buying, or of facilities for handling and storing—for him to lose money.

The subject of the storage and handling of wheat is one which does not carry its importance on the surface, the student or inexperienced young miller may feel inclined to treat it as unimportant—indeed the trade, as a whole, may be said to have been slow in grasping its possibilities for reducing expenses, but the up-to-date miller knows that his facilities for wheat handling and his system of storage have for him a great economic significance.

As in practically every other department of milling, the methods now obtaining for storing and handling wheat differ radically from those adopted in former times. But in this case the complete conversion of the trade to the new system came late, and it may be said that the necessity for the adoption of completely automatic grain handling plants has been only generally recognised since the beginning of the new century. Before that time there were, of course, a good many of the larger port mills equipped with labour-saving devices, but a majority of the members of the trade took a considerable time to see the savings that could be effected in labour, and in time by a capital outlay on a grain handling plant.

This subject divides itself into two parts (a) the handling (b) the storage.

The transport of wheat may be considered in connection with the methods for getting the wheat into the store—the "intake"—as it is in this direction that the greatest economies have been effected. Included in this, too, are the rest of the ordinary methods of transporting grain as far as they affect the miller. The original method of taking in wheat was to hoist the sack of grain up into the mill or warehouse, and the wheat was then stored either in the original sacks or shot by hand into a bin, or "started" (spread out) upon the granary floor. It should be noted that the bins of former days were open-topped, broad and comparatively shallow, and were neither expected nor suited to hold large quantities of grain. Big quantities of wheat were usually stored in bulk on floors and from time to time were "turned" by manual labour.

If the mill were situated on a riverside or by a quay and grain arrived in bulk, in the old days it was first of all bushelled into sacks and then hoisted up as before. With the arrival of automatic roller-process milling and an ever-increasing stress of competition, this method was found to be too expensive, and more or less automatic handling systems began to be used. In time the hoist was replaced in all merchant mills by the elevator, the sack truck by travelling band, the bushel measure by the ship elevator, the beam scale by the automatic weigher and the broad granary floor by the small deep silos.

The automatic plants in use at the present time discharge large vessels containing thousands of quarters of grain in less time than was taken to work out a barge under the old system.

Simultaneously with automatic handling, preliminary cleaning was developed. This has in some slight degree been made necessary by the difference in the mode of storing grain. Stored in silos 80 feet deep, the grain would be liable to deteriorate if all the dirt and dust were allowed to lie with it, to say nothing of the insufferable amount of dust that would be liberated every time the wheat came to be moved. Accordingly all mills of large and medium size have more or less extensive preliminary cleaning plants. Lastly automatic scales were introduced to weigh the wheat into the receiving house and at various stages during the cleaning, so that the miller knew exactly how much wheat was delivered to him and could estimate his loss from dirt and rubbish.

The extent of the intake plant will vary according to the size of the mill and the ideas of the owner, but the equipment of an average port or large mill will be somewhat as follows :—The ship or barge as it comes alongside the receiving house will be discharged by means of a " large " ship elevator. This is adjustable—that is to say, it can be raised or lowered according to the state of the tide or the amount of the grain in the hold. This elevator usually discharges on to large band conveyors, which take the wheat to the main inside elevator of the silo house. Thence it is elevated to the top of the mill and after being automatically weighed, it passes to the preliminary cleaning plant. In many mills this latter consists merely of a warehouse separator and a big fan which exhausts the wheat at various points. The warehouse separator is a machine of large capacity and designed merely to take out coarser impurities, dirt and sand, a powerful exhaust being applied both at the head and tail of the machine. In other mills the warehouse separator is preceded by a rubble-reel—a wire-covered machine, which tails over any large refuse, sticks and stones, and sifts out more dust—and is followed by another separator. A few millers indeed have even more elaborate preliminary cleaning plants at this stage. In all cases an exhaust is applied to the wheat at all possible points right from the time it leaves the ship elevator until it reaches the silos, so that the grain may have a thorough aeration and as much dust as possible may be eliminated at once. The capacity of intake plants varies. A medium-sized mill may have a plant capable of discharging a vessel, or barge, at the rate of 30 to 40 tons per hour, while some of the largest port mills have 150 tons per hour elevators and plant.

During the last few years pneumatic systems of grain handling and wheat intake have been introduced. By means of steam a powerful vacuum is induced. Armoured hose of considerable diameter are thrust into the grain in bulk as it lies in the vessel to be discharged, and are connected with a central receiving chamber. The vacuum causes the wheat to rush up the hose and into the receiving chamber, from whence it is discharged on to bands as before. Special air-locking devices prevent the vacuum being broken. In some cases the grain is transported all the way to the first weigher by the pneumatic system, the description given applies, of course, only to the discharging or intake elevator. This method, which is more expensive to install than the ordinary one, has several advantages. In the first place it takes less room; it is claimed, too, that the bottoms of vessels can be cleared more thoroughly and economically than with the ship elevator. Thirdly, the aeration is very good, for much dirt and dust are sucked out of the wheat at this first stage.

The pneumatic system is in operation at several of the largest port granaries and at a few mills. The expensiveness and the extra power needed to operate this system have, no doubt, prevented its extended use. Where both systems are installed, the pneumatic hose is usually brought into action to clear up a cargo, as it does this very quickly and economically, and thus the necessity for trimmers is obviated. Pneumatic transport has also been introduced with success where it is impossible either by reason of lack of space or for any other cause to install the ordinary band conveyors. Grain can sometimes be moved in this way dustlessly and without loss, where otherwise it might be impossible automatically to transport it at all.

In smaller mills the intake arrangements are not of so elaborate a character. At the same time there is practically always a central elevator with dumping pit attached, into which the wheat is pitched as it comes to the mill. From there it usually passes over an automatic weigher, and a warehouse separator before being sent to the silos, and thus in these cases, too, manual labour is reduced to a minimum.

Such very briefly is an outline of the methods employed in the intake and handling and preliminary cleaning of wheat. It has been thought superfluous to describe in detail either elevators or band conveyors, as the youngest miller is more or less acquainted with them.

After passing the intake plant, the wheat goes to the storage silos.

When writing about wheat storage it is no longer necessary to discuss whether or not it is more profitable to store wheat in bins or upon floors. The question is now decided, and every new mill now trusts for its storage space, practically to silos alone. The term " silo " is usually taken to mean either the building in which the dirty wheat is stored, or, in the plural, the bins themselves. It is hardly necessary to say that a silo consists of a number of bins, comparatively small and narrow in diameter, but deep. The reason for the large number of small bins is that thereby the wheat does not accumulate in too large a mass, many different parcels can be stored at the same time, and all be under perfect control. Practically speaking, silos may be constructed either (a) of interlaced wood (b) of steel (c) of brick and (d) of ferro-concrete. In this country neither steel nor brick silos are often erected, and interlaced wood and ferro-concrete hold the field, the former style being the one usually adopted for small mills, and the latter for large. Viewed purely from the point of view of keeping the wheat in good milling condition, the wood-wall silos are, perhaps, the best as they maintain the wheat in good condition, and the walls of the bins do not sweat, wood being a bad conductor of heat a fairly even temperature is maintained inside the bins. Besides this the interlacing makes the wood walls strong and fairly well able to resist the side thrusting stresses which are set up when the silos are full. On the other hand, an outside structure has to be built round them, and allowance must be made for the bins shrinking in height and warping somewhat, while they are not absolutely vermin proof. Last and perhaps most important, as recent events have shown, wood silos are not by any means fire proof, nor for storing big quantities of grain are they as strong or as economical as the other types.

Steel silos can be erected fairly cheaply and quickly. They are not, however, popular in this country. They are usually of considerable size, resembling huge steel cylinders set on end, so that they are only adapted for large parcels of grain. Their chief drawback, however, perhaps is that they are liable to sweat themselves, while steel, being a good heat conductor, any changes in outside temperature are communicated to the grain, which thus may easily be sent out of condition if stored in them in large bulks for a long time.

Brick silos have been used with satisfactory results, though brick work is not adapted to resist the side thrusts that are set up in a silo, and at the present time ferro-concrete is by far the most popular material to use for the erection of silos on a large scale. In the first place ferro-concrete silos are generally economical to construct and durable when constructed. Then, too, buildings of this material can be of any size or shape. The bins, of course, are many in number, and are generally about ten feet square, or ten feet by twelve feet. The depth of the silos varies from 60 feet to—in a few cases- - 120 feet. Ferro-concrete has many advantages, of which the greatest—cheapness and durability—have already been mentioned. Its resistance to the side strains and shifting masses of grain is very great; lastly, and very importantly, the concrete silo is practically fire proof, and in a place where of necessity there must be a greater or less quantity of dust in the atmosphere, in view of the constant risk of fire, a fireproof wheat store is a great asset.

Wheat, too, keeps its condition in this style of silos. They are not liable to sweat, and changes of temperature are only transmitted slowly. Altogether for silos of large capacity ferro-concrete is now being largely used. In small mills, or where silos have to be put inside an existing building, wood-wall bins are generally adopted, while, on account of their being easy to construct and their good storing qualities already mentioned, the conditioning, grinding and other incidental bins are practically always made of interlaced wood.

The strains and stresses that are set up by lateral pressure of the grain on the walls of the bins are always great and in large, deep silos are enormous. Great care must be taken when designing the silos to ensure that proper allowance is made for the lateral pressure, or " side bursts " may take place when the silos are full. The continual shifting of the weights of grain, as the wheat is moved in and out of the bins, also puts great alternating strains upon the silo house and its foundations.

A word about the equipment of the silo house may not be out of place. To the machinery of the intake plant reference has already been made. The wheat, as it leaves the intake plant, is discharged on to large travelling bands and from those—by means of throw-off carriages—it can be deflected into any required bin. Underneath the hoppers are other bands to take the wheat into the wheat-cleaning department. In small silo houses there is no need for conveyor bands over the top of the silos as the latter can be fed direct from the elevator, while for conveying wheat a few feet worm conveyors are sometimes employed.

Automatic weighers are often used to weigh the wheat both before and after the preliminary cleaning, as well as after the wheat-cleaning plant.

The dust plant needs some mention. From the nature of things a great deal of dust is necessarily liberated when dirty wheat is being moved, and an intake plant has yet to be evolved which will wholly prevent dust arising when many kinds of foreign wheat are being received into the mill. At the same time there are methods which can, to a great extent, overcome the nuisance and prevent the dust from permeating the building. Perhaps the best way is to have a strong, central fan and an exhaust nozzle drawing away dust wherever the wheat comes into the open air, i.e., at the feed and delivery of each machine, at the head or foot of the elevator, and as the wheat is being delivered to and from the bands and into the silo. A general exhaust on the silos is advisable in order to ensure ventilation. The pneumatic intake system, too, is very valuable in reducing the dust nuisance, while it cannot be doubted that the extra aeration the wheat thus gets makes all for its benefit. The value of an early aeration is very great. Many samples of wheat that arrive at the mill have mixed with them a quantity of close clinging dirt that tends to produce a smell in the wheat; sometimes, too, there are incipient growths of smut or other fungi and sometimes insects, such as weevils, are present. In any case, if the wheat is to be kept in the best condition, as many as possible of these impurities must be extracted at once; if this be done, the wheat will be the better, the subsequent machines will have less work to do, and will do what remains more efficiently.

The principles governing the storage of wheat must not be overlooked. In the time of our fathers, who used much more soft and comparatively damp wheat than is now the custom, and who, besides using native wheats, imported large quantities of soft wheat from the Continent, and soft American sorts, such as Michigan and White Canadian, the methods employed to keep these soft wheats in good milling condition were very carefully thought out. The soft wheats were not allowed to be together in too great bulk, they were constantly moved and aerated, and often mixed with dry, assimilative wheats in order that the tendency to heat or to go sour or out of condition, might be overcome. At the present time most of the foreign wheats arriving at the mill have comparatively a low moisture content, so that they can be stored in bins and, notwithstanding their considerable mass, they do not easily go out of condition. At the same time they should not be left too long in one bin, particularly if the parcel be a dirty one, containing a quantity of clinging dirt, such as is often found in Russians, or if there be any suspicion of smut. In such cases the wheat should be repeatedly moved, and thus in the journey from one bin to another it gets aerated, cooled, and sweetened—especially if there happens to be installed a central exhaust of the kind mentioned above. When English wheat has to be stored, care must be taken with it if it is excessively damp or has been badly harvested as it may get hot or acquire an offensive smell, or even become unusable. In storing native grain a favourite method is to spread it upon a floor and continually turn it, as was universally done in the old days. Where this is impossible and it must be stored in bins, too great a quantity should not be put in the same bin, while it should be kept continually moving. If the English wheat be damp and a little out of condition, but otherwise good, it is doubtful whether it is possible to improve on the old-fashioned way of mixing it, and letting it lie for a while with a dry wheat that easily assimilates moisture. This method requires some time, which is a drawback, but the results are often better than when the faulty English has been merely put through a drier. Speaking generally, hot air is hardly an ideal corrective for wheats that are out of condition, though sometimes its use is imperative.

In general, however, if reasonable precautions be taken, the storage of wheat does not cause the miller much trouble. Of the foreign sorts Russians, some Manitobas and occasionally Plates require the most careful watching. Of course, any parcels in which there is any trace of smut, or heat produced during the voyage, may give trouble as may any in which there are to any extent either refuse or weevils. Apart from these possible sources of danger, however, the work is not difficult.

Automatic milling has displaced the old-time systems, so automatic grain handling and storage demonstrates its economy over the old-time methods of moving grain.

THE PREPARATION OF WHEAT.

DRY CLEANING.

With the entry of the wheat into the screenhouse, what may be termed the ordinary cycle of milling operations begins. The great principle underlying the whole of these operaticns is separation; in the screenroom the wheat is separated from extraneous matter, in the mill the flour is separated from the offal. Both in the screenroom and the mill, the natural differences in size, in specific gravity, and in shape, between the many products that are fed into the various machines, are made by the miller to assist him to effect his separations. Wheat preparation divides itself into two divisions, viz., dry cleaning, and the washing and conditioning. Since the advent of roller milling the innovations that have been introduced into the principles of wheat cleaning have been mainly concerned with the washing and conditioning part of the process. The machinery now used for cleaning wheat dry, although, of course, it has been improved in the details of its construction, does not differ materially from that in use a score or more years ago. Of course, with regard to washing and conditioning, the situation is altogether different, but a consideration of that part of the mill must, for the moment, be deferred.

Only rarely have millers made any departure from the usual lines of arrangement of cleaning machines. One cleaning plant is very much like another, excepting a few accessories. No space need be taken up with a description of the machines, but some few lines may be devoted to the principles upon which the successful working of the plant depends.

Here, in parenthesis, for the benefit of the young miller, the fact may be emphasised that the various milling processes are so dependent upon one another that a mistake early in the system often may be traced right through to the flour sack. To take an obvious example, many have tried at some time or another and failed to lift impurities out of purifier feeds that would never have been in them if the cockle cylinders had been properly handled. This is an illustration, ready to hand, of the truism which says that no detail in the handling of milling machinery can be looked upon as unimportant. Considering first the milling separator, the machine calls for little notice. All the operative can do is to keep the meshes of the sieves clean and regulate the air valves. With regard to air valves, the wider they can be kept open at this stage the better, as thus the greater part of the screenings and dust is at once got away from the grain. The amount of draught that can safely be applied varies, of course, according to the sample and variety of the wheat being cleaned, the wheat that is merely dusty seldom causes bother, but rough samples of Plate or Russian often give the screensman great trouble. After the milling separator the wheat is treated in the barley and cockle cylinders. In large plants, graders usually size the wheat for the cylinders. In some cases the wheat, after being divided, goes through both sets of cylinders, in others the large wheat is treated only by the barley cylinders, the small by the cockle cylinders, while the medium grains alone go through both sets. In this way the number of cylinders is reduced.

The cylinders are, perhaps, the most important machines of the dry-cleaning system. They certainly require the most attention, any carelessness in handling cannot be explained away, and the most ingenious of screensmen will be unable to shake the witness of the small heavy black specks in the purifier feeds when comes his time of reckoning with the powers that be. As a rule, the cockle and seed separators will be more difficult to adjust than the barley cylinders, largely because of the difficulty of separating the round seeds from the wheat without taking out the broken grains. The installation of re-cockle and re-barley cylinders greatly assists the operative in effecting complete separations. The ordinary practice is so to set the primary cylinders that there is no chance of any impurities passing them. As a result a little wheat is taken out with the barley or seeds, but this is recovered on the secondary cylinders, and with the help of this method very discriminating separations can be effected by a skilled man. In all the best makes of cylinders the indents are drilled, and care needs to be taken to see that the covers are renewed whenever they become worn, for economies in this direction are apt to be expensive.

When once cylinders have been adjusted they will usually remain in position for as long as required, and as long as the class of wheat remains the same they need not be re-set. Speaking generally, Russian will be far the most difficult wheat to deal with at this stage as it generally contains cockle and small seeds and rape, buckwheat, barley and sometimes rye. When a bad sample is encountered, the only thing to do is to examine all the cylinders in turn to see that the best work possible under the circumstances is being effected. Rye, too, is very difficult to eliminate; special cyilnders are made to deal with it and big plants usually have an installation of them, but many mills do not have them, and in such cases samples of wheat containing rye should be avoided, as this cereal effects the baking properties of the flour, making it soft and unreliable.

The scourer usually follows the cylinders, but sometimes this machine is put after the conditioning process and millers are fairly evenly divided as to the merits of the respective positions. The washer and whizzer now perform some of the work formerly accomplished by the scourer. Millers who place the scourer after the conditioning bins say that a better polish and finish can be given to the wheat. On the other hand, it is argued that the wheat, after being washed, is in a very sensitive condition and that the last thing it should undergo is the violence of scouring, which may so abrade the bran as to produce a sensible loss. On the whole, the latter view predominates and the scourer is placed before the conditioning process rather more often than after it. Emery scourers are in great favour as they give the wheat a fine polish and help to loosen smut or hard dirt, so that the work of the washer is made much easier, while the wheat is not knocked about so much as in some of the older types of machines in which metal beaters alone do the scouring. After leaving the scourer (before washing), the wheat has passed through all the ordinary dry-cleaning machines and is next treated on the washing and conditioning plant.

Wheat, after being dried, is in a very sensitive condition. It is always liable to shed bran dust whenever it is moved. The brush machine is therefore inserted to give it a final polish before being sent to the grinding bins. The modern brush machine is often mounted on ball bearings and in this way power is saved, while as there is no great strain on the bearings, the wear is little. If the brushes be well set, the beard and any abraded bran will be removed from the wheat, which will then have a glistening smooth appearance and be less liable to shed more dust when subsequently moved. Between the grinding bins and the first break there is sometimes quite an array of machines, and sometimes none. In most mills, however, there is an automatic weigher, a steamer for occasional use, and a magnetic separator, while at some point there is an exhaust on the wheat. These machines are occasionally supplemented by a fine milling separator and another brush. The use of too many machines at this stage is hardly advisable, as the less moving the wheat has, after being cleaned and conditioned, the better. An exhaust on the grain, as the latter is being delivered into the first break feed hopper, is, however, very useful and has been found in some cases perceptibly to improve the colour of the first break stock. The whole point in applying the exhaust is to apply it at the last possible moment before the wheat goes on to the feed rolls, so that the wheat may drop into the nip of the rolls absolutely dustless.

Preceding the first break, magnets are usually installed. These may be of the ordinary horse-shoe type inserted in a spout, or instead the wheat may be fed in a thin stream over a magnetised steel plate, or an electric magnet may be preferred to either of the other types. The horse-shoe magnets do not make such certain separations as the other types and are apt to cause chokes in the spouts. In the other types there is usually an automatic cleaner to take away any pieces of metal that have been arrested. Magnets are often placed just before the scourer in order to obviate any chance of a spark being caused by the violent action of that machine. They are very useful accessories to the cleaning system; the amount of metal that is arrested by them is often considerable, and is an ample justification for their inclusion.

THE PREPARATION OF WHEAT.

WHEAT WASHING AND CONDITIONING.

THE MOISTURE CONTENT—CAUSES OF VARIATION.

The washing and conditioning department of the mill has for many years been recognised as second only in importance to the flour mill itself. During the last two decades the washing of all foreign wheat has become almost general, while the practice of wheat conditioning is now regarded as a scientific operation. The study of the results of immersing wheat in water is most fascinating, for in this section of the milling system, notwithstanding the ingenuity and labour which have been expended upon it, there is still room for improvement, and, as recent events in the milling world have shown, the last word on this topic has not yet been said. Indeed at the present time there are considerable changes taking place in this department.

The miller, when washing and conditioning wheat, has three main objects in view. (1) He reckons on thoroughly cleaning the wheat; (2) he attempts to bring it into the best possible condition for milling; (3) in a few cases he is able to add a little moisture to the endosperm. The third of these objects is in many cases an incidental effect of conditioning, and is in the ordinary way subservient to the second, though there are millers to be found who work on the principle that the proper amount of moisture for any wheat is the utmost it will carry without hopelessly choking the mill.

With regard to cleaning wheat by washing not much need be said, except that many wheats would practically be unusable were it not for the existence of the washing plant. Immersion in water also is the only known satisfactory method of separating stones from wheat. The principle governing the action of a stoner is identical with that of the exhaust in a wheat-cleaning machine; that is to say, in each case the separation is effected by taking advantage of the difference in the specific gravity between wheat and its impurities. In the case of the exhaust air is a differentiating medium, in the case of the washer water. The governing idea is the same for all washers and stoners. The wheat and stones are fed into a current of water; the wheat, being only slightly heavier than the water, sinks but slowly and is carried along by the current, while the stones, being heavy, sink at once and can be collected in a special receptacle. In different machines various mechanical arrangements assist the separations, the main principle, however, is in every case the same. One or two machines carry the principle still further and float off any light screenings or refuse. In such cases the washer differentiates between three different specific gravities. The washer and whizzer, too, are the only effective machines for treating smutty or evil smelling wheat and for such samples these machines do effectively what the scourer used to do indifferently. The difficulty with many smutted samples is that the smut clings very tightly and much water and hydro scouring is needed to remove it, therefore the grain absorbs too much moisture and needs extra drying to bring it back to a milling condition. When the miller starts to accomplish his second object, viz., the conditioning as distinguished from the cleaning of the wheat, then he finds himself at the "beginning of tribulations." The problem the mill manager and screensman are set to solve is this : In an average merchant mill's wheat mixture there is a number of wheats of various kinds. Each of these sorts differ in many respects from all the others; each has a different natural moisture content, each, to a greater or less degree, behaves differently when passing the washing plant; some kinds of wheat absorb water quickly, some slowly, some need a lot of water, some a little, and yet all the various wheats of a mixture when they come to the first break should have an even condition and "temper" and break down under the rolls in a free manner without cutting up the bran. To get a number of wheats to a uniform condition, such as this, is not altogether easy. Each day's work may in itself be good, but, taken together, two days' work may not be good and for this reason. Every time the amount of moisture is materially altered, although the condition of the grain is perfect, the resultant flour might also be altered. The laundry process introduces fluctuations in quality more quickly and quietly than any section of the mill. Unfortunately, the direct cause of these fluctuations is difficult to fathom, though excessive duration of the immersion of the wheat is generally to blame. Sometimes slipping belts cause the volume of air being blown through the drier to alter and thus there are fluctuations in the amount of moisture carried off. The temperature of the hot air is difficult to keep constant, and this is another source of trouble. Again it is impossible to keep the interval between washing and grinding quite fixed and big variations here will mean variations in the work of the mill. Finally, the vagaries of the English weather add to the difficulties of the situation. On a dry day the atmosphere will carry off much more moisture than when the air is humid. The method usually adopted by the screensman to prevent these variations is to make continual tests on the work being done and to note the results down, so that a comparison of them with those of the day before can be made. The chief of these tests consists in weighing a known volume of wheat, say, a quart—at regular intervals as it leaves the whizzer or the drier. In this way, although the exact moisture content cannot be determined, any variations from normal washing can be at once detected. This method is employed in most mills. In addition, of course, the exact moisture content of all wheats is regularly determined before and after conditioning. This, however, takes some little time, while the weighing of a quart of wheat takes but a minute.

The exact actions that are set up inside the berry by conditioning are not, even at the present time, completely understood; speaking generally, however, it may be said that the effect of moisture and heat is to start a process of very light fermentation, this affects the flavour of the flour, and if the wheat be milled at the proper time a sweet flavour is transmitted to the flour; if, however, the wheat is left too long before being milled the good effects are lost and instead a secondary acid fermentation is set up which is detrimental to the flavour of the flour. Under various systems of conditioning different intervals between washing and grinding are found to be the most suitable. Various wheats, of course, differ from each other in the time they require to be left in the conditioning bins. In every case, however, the capable screensman endeavours to adhere as far as possible to the interval which is found by experiment to be the most advantageous.

A word or two may be inserted with regard to the use of hot air. In view of the fact that it is liable to set up chemical actions that cannot be controlled, millers at the present time are usually somewhat sparing in their use of hot air, and in this respect there is some reaction from the methods of a few years ago when hot air was much more frequently used than is now the custom. As a rule, at the present time, a large volume of cold air is preferred to the use of any hot air for drying the grain. One other point may be mentioned in this direction, as hot air has always to be heated artificially, usually by steam from the boiler, its cost in the course of a year is considerable and appreciably adds to the cost of working the wheat-cleaning plant. As a matter of fact there are plenty of mills which have neither dryer nor cooler and which allow the wheat to dry in the conditioning bins. Such mills can use ordinary wheats with excellent results, but if wheats needing special treatment are to be milled they are handicapped. On the other hand, hot air is of service to the miller when very hard or unassimilative wheats have to be treated, and in such cases their value can be greatly enhanced by the use of hot air or hot water, for the harshness of the class of wheat is mellowed, and its " temper " improved.

Present practice favours the later " radiator " type of conditioner, and in this make of machine the application of heated air by fan draught is being discontinued.

The student is frequently asked whether it is better to wash wheats separately or in a mixture. The question is a very hardy perennial at the milling examinations. Theoretically, every wheat should be treated alone, and on its merits. Practically, however, this is often impossible, at any rate when there are a number of different wheats in a mixture, as bin space and time often will not allow. In such a case wheats that behave alike in the bath are grouped and worked together or else some very peculiar results may be obtained. A concrete example may illustrate the point. Suppose, for instance, a mixture contains Manitobas, Russians, Australians, Kurrachee and English, the proportions are immaterial for the moment. If all these wheats were mixed together and washed, given an average immersion and an interval in the conditioning bins, the mill staff would have interesting experiences when they milled the mixture. It has to be borne in mind that time is the controlling factor in conditioning. The longer the time available for tempering by contact in the conditioning bin after washing, the more independent can one be of the grouping system. For Manitobas take only a moderate amount of water and that rather slowly, Russians need thorough washing and drying, Australians take water very fast and may easily become water-logged. Kurrachees need washing at least twice with a considerable interval between the immersions, and even then they assimilate the moisture slowly. English is hardly ever improved by washing and unless very smutty had much better be treated dry. The result of mixed washing and conditioning would be that the Manitobas would be in fair condition, the Russians would not have had a thorough enough drying, the Australians would have too much moisture, the Kurrachees would hardly be mellowed at all, while the English would be far too damp. In practice the English would probably be treated dry, and other sorts separately. If this were impracticable, the Kurrachees, after having a preliminary soaking and being allowed to lie awhile in the tempering bins, might be rewashed with the Russians. The Manitobas would require some little time for the moisture thoroughly to permeate them; the Australians, on the other hand, absorb moisture so quickly that they would need only a short immersion or time in the bins. By this means the mixture should go to the first break in uniform condition. Two things will be found difficult to compass, firstly to determine exactly how long the moisture will take to permeate the berry evenly and, secondly, to ensure that the whole mixture shall be of even temper. It need hardly be said that it is perfectly possible to have all the wheats go on the mill containing a perfectly equal percentage of moisture, and yet for them to be in thoroughly irregular milling condition. For an example the hypothetical mixture may once more be considered. All the foreign wheats may have a uniform moisture content, and yet the mixture is not necessarily in good milling condition. The Kurrachees and Russians may have been sent on to the mill rather too soon; in that case their moisture content may be right, but the bran will be tough, and the middle of the grain hard and dry, with the result that patents obtained from the mixture will be off colour. If the Australian wheat be kept too long, just the opposite will happen. The moisture will be mostly in the endosperm, and consequently there will be a lot of high-coloured break flour, but only comparatively few high-class middlings. The condition for a mixture should be such that all the grains are of equal temper, the bran tough, and the whole mixture breaks down easily under the rolls, while at the same time a maximum quantity of semolina and middlings is released. Some millers have gone a step further in the conditioning process and give to each wheat the degree of moisture which gives the best baking results. Regulating the moisture contents of the flour according to the needs of the baking process and not to suit the milling of it is an art that is imperfectly understood as yet, but there is no doubt that flour requires a different percentage of moisture for producing the best possible baking results to that required by the wheat to make it in what we call perfect condition. This method of conditioning will again be referred to when the third phase of the process is considered.

One of the greatest aids to successful conditioning is the regular keeping of as many records as possible. If a record be kept of the wheats used, their moisture content and natural weight before and after treatment, the time between washing and grinding, and the temperature of the air draughts together with a few brief notes of the baking qualities of the flour, in a surprisingly short time there will be collected a mass of data on the subject of conditioning which will be considerable.

A few notes may be appended with regard to wheats requiring special treatment. The Indians as a class, perhaps, require the most attention from the conditioning department. Probably the secret of success in treating them is to begin soon enough. They may be well damped two or three times with an interval between each operation. The judicious use of steam and hot water, too, greatly mellow their natural harshness, and some millers after washing them with all the water possible inject a jet of live steam into the hot air of the drier, and shut off the cold air and then run the wheat straight to the conditioning bin, in this way the flavour as well as the temper of the wheat is said materially to be improved. The same treatment can be given to Durum should that wheat appear on the English market. Plates also need a word or two. They do not take up a great quantity of water, but the skin dries very quickly on the outside, so that the wheat often appears ready for the mill soon after being washed. On the other hand, the moisture takes some little time to permeate the grain, so that the quickness in assimilating moisture is more apparent than real.

With regard to the third object for which the miller washes his wheat, namely, the addition of moisture, a change in method appears to be taking place. As has been pointed out, during conditioning, it is very difficult to add more than a small extra percentage to the endosperm of the wheat. The effect, too, of milling a mixture with very high moisture content has sometimes been seen in the offals becoming heated when stored and much loss from evaporation in the mill. The stocks, too, are a little apt to sweat, and in addition there is the difficulty of getting uniformity in the distribution of the moisture throughout the berry. This has been recognised, and consequently extra heavily-conditioned mixtures are not now in such favour as they were a few years ago. At the same time there can be no doubt that the addition of a little moisture to the endosperm of the wheat during the process of conditioning or milling, besides incidentally bringing a slight direct profit to the miller, stimulates the enzymes and promotes some action among the constituents of the flour that has the effect of improving it. Until a short time since the only means of adding this moisture was by washing, although as has been noted this, though a serviceable and practicable, is not an ideal method. Recently, however, millers have had an alternative offered to them. The alternative method consists of adding moisture to the middlings during the process of milling, in the form of a very finely-divided spray. There are two or three spraying systems in the market, the principle, however, in every case is the same. By means of these sprayers soluble flour improvers and yeast foods can also be added to the flour and middlings, but a consideration of flour improving and treatment does not now arise, it is as adjuncts to conditioning that spraying systems have now to be considered. In parenthesis it may be noted that the spray consists of moisture so finely divided as to resemble wet mist. The spraying can be and is done at several points in the milling system, but the most usual plan is to spray the semolina and middlings after being purified and before passing the reduction rolls. The feeds of the lower reductions or even the flour itself can, if necessary, be subjected to the spray.

Those millers who favour this new system argue that several advantages are to be gained by its use. It is asserted first that the addition of the very finely-divided moisture to the middlings, even without any improver being contained in solution, has the effect of improving the baking qualities of the resultant flour. In addition the mill is said to run cooler, less power being required to reduce the middlings which have been softened, while the ordinary loss by evaporation is over-come. In addition to this, when working the wheat the miller need aim merely at getting the mixture into the best condition for a heavy release of semolina and middlings from the breaks and need not trouble about the last one per cent. to be added to the endosperm. At the present time it is perhaps too early to assume that every one of the above assertions has been proved, although a number of large mills have installed the new system, but there can be no doubt that it attracts, and that the idea of adding the last one per cent. of water to the middlings in the mill considerably simplifies the work of the man in charge of the washer. For it is the last one per cent. of added moisture which, though necessary if the best results are to be obtained, gives the greatest trouble to the screensman and the mill staff. The fact, too, that loss by evaporation during milling is greatly reduced by the new process will also doubtless commend it to millers.

Reverting for one moment to the underlying principle of all successful conditioning, it may once more be repeated that uniformity of work from day to day is essential to successful conditioning. The point can hardly be laboured too much, for every change in the moisture content, or the condition of the wheat means that the working of the mill, its capacity, its percentages, the baking properties of the flour, and the quality of the offals will all be affected to a greater or less degree.

THE WHEAT MIXTURE.

AIMS OF THE MILLER.

To a great extent the state of a miller's balance-sheet depends upon the proper selection and purchase of the wheat for the mixture. No other single phase of the business has, to anything like an equal extent, so direct an influence on the profits. In choosing the wheats for his mixture, the miller's technical knowledge and his business ability are alike called into play. His technical knowledge is needed to tell him what result he may expect in the loaf from a given sample of wheat; his business ability to enable him to judge the most opportune moment for a purchase, or the true value of the parcel he contemplates buying. The tendency of the milling trade for some time has been more and more to emphasise the importance of the wheat buyer. In times past the head of a large firm of millers, as a matter of course, was conversant with every detail of his mill, and every characteristic of each of his employees. But the present is an age of specialists and big firms, consequently to-day in our large merchant mills the technical and commercial staffs are kept quite distinct, while the head of the firm, practically by necessity, devotes the greater part of his energies to the buying, and leaves the details of the mill's working to the mill manager and staff. Putting aside for the moment the question of profit, the character of the products of the mill must naturally depend upon the character of the wheats milled.

The world's wheats in their season are at the service of the English miller, and his task is to blend them so that their various qualities shall combine to produce a good flour and at the same time yield a satisfactory profit. In respect of the number of wheats from which he may make his blend, the

English miller occupies an unique position among the millers of the world. In no other country are such varied mixtures regularly to be found as in England, and in no other country is any lapse from high quality visited with greater severity upon the offending miller. Thus, for instance, the average United States miller usually grinds either all spring or all winter wheat and only occasionally a mixture of the two. The Continental miller, too, hardly ever has such a varied assortment of wheats in his blend as is quite common in this country and accordingly his task is so much the simpler.

The buyer, when selecting the wheats for a mixture, has to keep before him a number of considerations. Firstly, he has to think of the quality of the resultant flour, or, more accurately, of the quality of the loaf the resultant flour will produce. He has to bear in mind the class of trade for which he intends to cater, and consequently the properties in regard to strength, colour and yield of the various wheats from which he may choose. Again he has to maintain the regularity of his flour. This sometimes is quite a serious difficulty, for, of course, the varieties available vary with the seasons, and there are often occasions when the wheats which are being depended upon to supply " backbone " to the mixture are too high in price to be used, yet this difficulty must be met, and in some manner overcome, for the one grade of flour for which bakers will accept no excuse, is the flour on which they cannot rely as being regular. They generally boycott a flour that one week gives them a splendid lot of bread, and the next a batch of defective loaves. And so it is an axiom with the miller that his flour must be kept regular, and, in a big mill where a large amount of flour may easily be spoilt in a few hours, many and elaborate are the precautions that are taken, in order that the flour may be kept regular. And while the miller is keeping all the above matters in his mind above everything hangs the question of profit, for profit, after all is what the miller is seeking. And it is the necessity of buy ing wheats that when mixed will not only yield good flour. but a fair profit that makes wheat mixing so difficult. It is com paratively easy to sketch out a good mixture—when always

68

buying the best wheats—as then the bakers will be pleased, the mill staff delighted and the percentage of flour excellent: in fact, everything will be well but the profits, which may often be non-existent.

In planning a mixture the style of flour required comes first for consideration—in this respect the millers of some districts are rather more favoured than are those of others, for, of course, the class of flour favoured by customers varies very considerably in different parts of the United Kingdom and even of England. Thus, for example, in London and the South, and in fact wherever bread is made by professional bakers, the miller has to provide a flour that, above everything, shall be strong and make handsome loaves, as well as a good number of them per sack. Further, the flour is expected to be of an average colour. Wherever home baking is the custom flour is not required to be of such great strength. Colour and flavour are then the first characteristics and as long as the loaf is of medium size consumers are satisfied. In Ireland there is a demand for flour of snowy whiteness; while in Scotland big loaves, often having a coarse texture, are preferred, such as may be obtained by baking strong flour alone. There are also numerous local preferences.

Having determined the class of flour he wishes to make, the miller has next to look round for the wheats with which to make it. It will not be necessary to review the qualities of the various wheats from which he can choose, as that has already been done. The miller who wishes to make a high-class flour will often have a difficult task, as the wheats of the best class often stand at such a figure that they are commercially unworkable. The question of flour yield is one of vital importance when buying wheat, though occasionally it is overlooked. It is well, too, to be precise as to what percentage is meant. Thus when speaking of the percentage obtained by the mill, millers often mean the percentages obtained from the clean wheat. As a matter of fact, however, the really important percentage is that obtained from the uncleaned sample. Needless to say a wheat, which when well cleaned gives a high yield of flour, does not necessarily come out well when tested by the yield of flour from the bulk sample.

The flavour of the bread has also to be taken into account in choosing a mixture, although it is not of such supreme importance as in former times. At one time the flavour was one of the chief characteristics to be considered when buying wheat, to-day the consuming public takes more notice of the appearance of a loaf than of its taste, but the latter must be passable or it would limit the demand. The laments about the absence of a nutty flavour in the bread of to-day, compared with that of two generations ago, are not much heeded as long as the loaf is fairly sweet. At the same time, millers—especially those in the country or where the housewife is the baker—still find that some attention must be paid to the flavour of their flour. In this respect the country miller can claim an advantage over the port miller, as the former usually has a large and handy supply of English wheat and this, for flavour, easily out-distances all its rivals. A few words may be inserted with regard to the use of the lower grades of well-known wheats. On certain occasions there are in the market large quantities of the lower grades of the strong wheats. The 1911 Canadian crop is a typical example, but every year there are to be obtained samples of low grade wheat and particularly of the lower grades of the strong varieties. They are, of course, obtainable at a much lower price than the higher or safer grades and so at times, when the miller is often hard put even to show a theoretical profit on his mixture, the sight of low-priced wheats which bear a name for strength is very tempting. Accordingly many millers have bought them and some have wished they had left them alone. Once in the mill they begin to be expensive. In the first place the cleaning loss is very apt to be greater than is expected, even when ample allowance has been made. Then a smaller flour percentage is naturally allowed for, but actual yields are astonishingly small when accurately tested, while the quality of the flour is below that obtained from the higher grades of the same wheat. The fact is the lower grades of Manitobas or such like wheats, must be treated as if they did not bear a well-honoured name. Their value in a mixture—except in very small proportions and after all allowances have been made—in any case is doubtful, for usually 60 per cent. of flour is all that can be expected from them, while in addition they must be conditioned very carefully, or they will be swamped. Their strength, on the other hand, is rather higher than their other qualities would seem to warwant, but unfortunately it is unreliable. One other point about them needs mention. It must be remembered that the presence of low grade wheats in any great proportion in a mixture lowers the capacity of the mill to a surprising degree, and consequently increases the cost of manufacture, since with the same expenses a longer time than usual is needed to make a sack of flour. It can thus be seen that wheat must stand at a very low figure to be profitable when allowances have to be made for 10 per cent. less flour, a double screening loss, less added moisture, extra cost of production and at the finish a poorer quality of flour. So much for the low grade wheats.

Reference has been made to the need for regularity in the flour. The difficulty of maintaining this will be apparent when any variety which has been regularly included in the mixture in large proportions becomes unavailable. During the last few years the number of wheats from which the miller could choose at a given time has tended to become rather smaller. The very strong wheats are the most difficult to replace. Of the wheats of medium strength simultaneously with the development of scientific methods of conditioning, Indians have rapidly advanced in the favour of millers. Some of them make quite a bulky, though coarse, loaf, but they also are liked, not only because they lend themselves to conditioning, but because they add a lot of what may be termed " Baker's Strength " to the mixture. This expression, perhaps, calls for explanation. Many bakers by a strong flour mean a flour that will take up a big amount of moisture and make a large number of loaves per sack; the miller calls a flour strong that makes a big shapely loaf. It is the former strength that is supplied in a pre-eminent degree by the hard

Indian wheats, even after thorough conditioning, and as a result these wheats help to make a flour popular with bakers in spite of an insipid flavour

With the above considerations in view a typically cosmopolitan English mixture may very briefly be examined and its composition analysed. Suppose, for example, a mixture made up as follows :—

20 Manitoba, No 2.
10 Russian.
15 Karachi.
5 No. 2 Club Calcuttas.
20 Plates (Rosafe 62 lbs.)
20 English.
10 Australian.
———
100

It will first of all be noticed that the really strong wheats are represented to the extent of 30 per cent. This makes a good solid foundation of strength for the mixture, especially as the Manitobas and Russians, though the strongest, are not the only wheats in the mixture which add to its strength. Of course, if all the other varieties had been of the weak type 30 per cent. of the extra strong wheats would not have been sufficient. But the Club, Plate and Kurrachee (putting them in the order of strength) will each carry itself and still have a little strength to lend to the weaker sorts, so that in all 70 per cent of the varieties in the mixture come under the category of strength. The weaker wheats are represented by English and Australian. The English will improve both the colour and flavour of the flour, and in addition will help to neutralise the tendency towards coarseness in the texture of the loaf, that may be set up by the large proportion of Indian and Manitoba that is present. The Australian adds '' class '' to the mixture and bloom to the flour and also materially helps the flour percentage. The Plate has been left to the last, but it is among the most useful of wheats in a mixture. It is '' safe '' for strength and will give a beautiful bloom and colour to the flour, particularly to the patents, and it has the further recommendation of working well in the mill.

Thus in the above mixture strength, colour and the bulking character of the flour have alike been considered, though naturally price, perhaps the most important of all the considerations, cannot here be taken into account. From such a mixture a high-class flour and a good length of patents well suited for bakers' breadmaking would be obtained.

The methods employed in the mill of blending the various sorts of wheat may be worth a very few words. Twenty years ago the almost universal method of making up the mixture was to shoot a sack of more of each sort in turn into the bin, so that the desired proportions were attained. This method is still pursued in a few mills, practically all of them, however, being only very small. This method had the advantage of being simple and further the wheats were mixed by weight, so that the exact proportions could be maintained. On the other hand, since such a considerable quantity of each variety was shot at a time, the wheat had a tendency to run in layers. Automatic methods, however, were finally responsible for the disappearance of this method and revolving mixers, which can be set to deliver the required proportions of wheat, are now all but universal. These mixers besides being automatic have the great advantage of mixing the wheats in small quantities, so that the different sorts of wheat may be blended quite evenly. It may be noted that, in the ordinary way these mixers measure the grain alone, and thus if there be wheats of greatly differing specific gravity in the mixture an element of error is introduced. In order to overcome this difficulty, some mixers are made which deliver by weight as well as by volume. The only danger with automatic mixers is that occasionally either by reason of the grain choking in the bin hoppers or spouts, or through a bin running empty unexpectedly because of carelessness, the mixer for a time may be turning but not delivering and thus the balance of the wheats in the mixture be lost. Automatic safeguards are usually installed in large plants to provide against this eventuality. They usually consist of bells arranged so that they ring immediately wheat ceases to be delivered to the mixer, or when one bin of wheat runs empty all the mixers are stopped electrically.

In conclusion, to sum up, it may agam be noted that, although much may be written about wheat blending, the two most essential objects are to keep the quality of the flour up to the standard, and the price of the mixture down. To do either separately is comparatively easy, but our most experienced millers find all their powers taxed to do both.

GRADUAL REDUCTION PROCESS.

ITS INCEPTION AND DEVELOPMENT.

Gradual reduction may well be termed the great foundation principle upon which the whole of the theory and practice of modern flour milling has been built. The whole essence of that theory and practice is that the complete separation of the flour from the husk of the wheat berry, shall be accomplished not in one, but after a number of successive operations and after passing many machines each of which has a special work to perform. Like several other of the great changes which have revolutionised more than a few of our manufacturing trades, the principle of gradual reduction was evolved as a commercial process during the middle part of the reign of Queen Victoria. The details of the milling system have since been improved, but the idea has never changed since it was first adopted. The development of the idea once it had been accepted by millers proceeded very rapidly, as the superiority of the flour made in mills erected on the new system literally compelled millers to adopt the new principle, though many of them in this country did so only after much hesitation and many misgivings. But before writing further of gradual reduction or the universally accepted bed rock foundation of milling technology, it may be well briefly to consider on what principles, flour milling, almost the most ancient of all industries, had been conducted before the new systems were invented.

The millstone, of course, was absolutely universal before the advent of the new systems. The art of stone milling was one that needed no little labour to acquire, and during the years immediately preceding its final abandonment, stone milling had been brought to the wonderful pitch of perfection. Most of the mills of this country were driven by either wind or water power and of comparatively small capacity, but there were also many large steam driven stone mills near the big towns, in which a very high degree of engineering skill could have been observed. And yet the interesting fact remains that the grinding appliances in England, in 1880, were on the same principle as those used in Oriental countries many centuries before. The fact is thus brought out that though from time to time the various details of the milling system were developed, yet, the root idea was left untouched and the general name " millstones " stood for the wheat grinders in every mill from the Victorian era right back to Biblical times. In practically every case the top stone revolved over a fixed bottom one, the wheat was fed into the eye of the stone, and the bran was sifted away from the flour by various means, the hand sieves of the earliest times being afterwards followed by mechanical sifters and flour-dressing machines.

Side by side with gradual reduction there has grown up with the new systems of milling another great basic principle without which milling on the scale pursued by our largest mills of to-day would have been impossible. The principle is perhaps less important than the one before referred to, but still, when first put into practice it was a great departure from the methods that had been practised from time immemorial. The principle in question is that of automatic working of all machinery, and of the handling of all the stocks in a flour mill by mechanical means. The introduction of automatic methods came rather later than the principle of gradual reduction; while the adoption of mechanical handling for practically everything that has to be moved in a flour mill—whether raw material, mill stocks, or finished products—is still in progress, as in only a portion of the mills is this system fully employed. These two principles differ from one another in that while the first—gradual reduction—affects the method of manufacture, and renders the miller able to make a better flour than he had previously been able to do, the second—automatism—is concerned merely with the economics of flour milling. At the present time the young miller is so accustomed to see the long row of elevators rising nearly to the full height of a mill, that it is not unnatural if he forgets not only how recently has automatic grain handling and automatic weighing and the like been introduced, but also how comparatively recent has been the adoption of automatic roller process flour milling itself. Sixty years ago there probably was not a single automatic roller mill in this or any other country. Most of the ten thousand British flour mills that then existed, were comparatively small, the motive power was the local mill-stream or the wind. In many of them a man and a boy were the sole employees. The wheat ground was mostly grown in the district, though towards the end of the stone milling era millers were compelled to use ever increasing proportions of stronger foreign wheats. In parenthesis, however, it may be said that the attempt to grind the brittle foreign wheats in large proportions between the stones marked the beginning of the end of the millstone system. The wheat in these old millstone mills was conveyed to the mill in the carters' and millers' trucks, then it was hoisted in sacks to the top of the building and shot into the feeding bin over the millstone. The meal as it emerged all hot from the stone fell into a cooling bin in the basement— usually open at one end to the rest of the floor. Thence the miller shovelled it into sacks, and with the help of his boy, hoisted it to the top of the mill, to stand until cool, and then a few days afterwards he shot it into a larger bin. From this large bin the meal was fed into a long cumbrous bolting-reel which was often the single flour-dressing, separating and scalping machine of the plant. A mere recital of these methods and a mental comparison with those in use in even the smallest modern roller mills, shows the difference which automatic methods have made. Even after the introduction of the principle of gradual reduction, which by reason of the fact that it multiplied the flour-making processes, rendered automatic methods necessary, it was some little time before automatic milling became universal even for roller plants. Indeed, several mills fitted wholly on the roller system were erected in this country on non-automatic lines, while to this day in Hungary mills making, perhaps, five breakings and double that number of reductions, can be found, in which the meal is caught off in sacks after each operation, and hoisted to the top of the mill before being sent to the purifiers or dressing machinery. However, speaking generally, it was not long after the introduction of the roller system before every British and American mill was perfectly automatic as regards the actual milling processes. Automatic grain handling, however, and the elimination of manual labour for the movement of the finished products, took longer to develop, and the movement in this direction has even now not been completed, but this extension of the principle of automatism has already been considered elsewhere. Suffice it to say that this principle is regarded as being right at the root of milling economics of the present day.

But to return to the parent principle of gradual reduction. The idea took some little time to develop. It was first introduced in connection with the millstone. The first signs of the changes which were afterwards to revolutionise milling can be traced back to the beginning of the second half of the nineteenth century. Various spasmodic departures had before been made from the principle of single grinding, but they had not been followed up, and it was only at that time that " high grinding " was first found to have commercial successful possibilities. The practice, however, spread, and towards the end of the fifties high grinding, used in conjunction with purifiers, began to be used in a fair number of mills on the Continent—notably in Hungary. Probably the first mill in which gradual reduction was attempted on an extended scale was the Walzmuhle, in Budapest, and in one or two of the mills in that city, rolls were certainly used about the year 1860, and it was not long before practically all the Pesth mills had adopted the gradual reduction system by means of rolls and stones, though it was some years afterwards before they were worked upon automatic lines. Some little time before this, in quite a number of Continental mills, rather primitive purifiers had been installed and the first pair of stones were set " high " so as to make middlings which were afterwards reduced on other stones. High grinding, however, did not come to this country until some years later and then only when the English milling trade was threatened, first by the competition of American *New Process* flour and then by *roller flour.*

English millers, as became their naturally conservative character, fought hard against the innovations. Many of them were convinced that, in the end, the stones with which they were so familiar would outlast both the new process and the roller systems. All of them were very loth to abandon the old stone milling system and the principles that governed it In defence of what may perhaps seem the slowness of the English millers to make the necessary changes, one fact must not be lost sight of. That is the public taste in bread had been altered by the light loaves produced from " New Process " foreign flour that was then being sent to this country. The English stone mills until a short time before the advent of the roller systems had ground principally English wheat, while the foreign varieties that were imported consisted chiefly of American Winters, Californian or European wheat. In either case the bulk of the imported and the native wheats which made up the mixture was mellow excepting that from California, which was of a ricey character. Only in quite small proportions did millers include the hard, brittle strong wheats, such as American Spring and Indian sorts. It can be seen at once that the stones, with their vigorous rasping action, would naturally do far better work on a tough mellow mixture of wheat than when attempting to clean up a hard, brittle-skinned mixture. The millers of Hungary, and afterwards those of America, commenced to export flour to this country. In both cases, apart from its other merits, the imported flour was much stronger than that which the English millers had been accustomed to make. The superiority, however, was seen to be remediable and the English millers began to make a flour that would compete with the foreign article, and in consequence had to grind a larger proportion of the strong foreign wheats. This practically drove the last nail in the coffin of the stone mill, for it had to attempt to compete with the new gradual reduction systems under the most unfavourable conditions. In the towns the stone mills would never have withstood the competition of the roller plants, but in many country districts the stone mills, though in the end the roller system would doubtless have proved omnipotent, might have been able to exist for much longer if it had not been found necessary to grind increasingly large quantities of the foreign wheat for which the stones were most unsuited. It is possible that if the present methods of washing and conditioning had then been known, the stone mills of this country might have been able to hold out considerably longer than they did. Whether, however, this would have been an ultimate benefit to the trade of this country, or whether it would have meant that English millers would have never regained their supremacy in the home markets, it is impossible to say.

So at last the English miller found that the harder foreign wheats could not by any means be reduced at one operation, if the resultant flour were to have any chance of competing with the roller-made product. Then all sorts of improvements and expedients were tried in order that the old mill stones which had been brought to a high pitch of perfection, might be retained in the milling systems. Many were the composite systems which were installed in English mills during this transitional period, but at last after a long time English millers found that they must either use rolls for all their wheat grinding processes or shut down their mills. The first turning point may be said to be marked by the exhibition of milling machinery at the Royal Agricultural Show, which took place at Kilburn, London, in 1879, but the main thing drawing millers attention to the roller system was the exhibition of milling machinery in London two years later. After 1881, the question of whether stones or rolls gave the best results could hardly be recognised as debatable, and the next few years saw the greater part of the large English mills converted to the roller process. In the country, stone mills lasted longer, though far-seeing men who could raise the necessary capital lost no time in adopting an up-to-date system. The way English millers set themselves to recover the trade they had lost, and the way they succeeded, though many a milling business fell in the struggle, is well known to most millers. It will, perhaps, suffice to say, that the roller system has become so firmly established that it would now be nearly as difficult to introduce another new system, as it was to convince millers of the worth of the roller system when it first appeared.

⋅ With regard to the principles of the roller system, it is rather singular how few changes have been made in the principles affecting the vital parts of the system. Thus to take an instance in point, the theory regarding breaking has never altered. The principle of cleaning the bran in a greater or less number of successive operations has always remained the same. The method of carrying out these principles, however, has differed very greatly from time to time. Grooved rolls, disintegrators, high-speed discs, various peculiarly constructed grinders, all these have been experimented with by English millers engaged in the search for an ideal break system. There have been as many as eight breaks and as few as two, while the grooving, differentials and speeds of the various rolls have fluctuated greatly according to the fashion of the time. The central principle, however, has remained the same amid all these changes.

One change only has taken place in the process of flour manufacture which can be said really vitally to have affected the principles upon which millers work. With regard to the condition and temper in which wheat is milled, there is a radical difference between the treatment wheat now receives and that which it received during the earlier years of roller milling. The discovery that practically all foreign wheat in its natural state is not in an ideal state for milling, and the universal adoption of wheat washing has had more far reaching effects than any other change that has come over milling since the introduction of rolls. The conditioning of wheat has become practically a science, and the addition of moisture to the berry, when properly carried out, is now universally recognised as an indispensable aid to profit making. The

refinement of practice and the exact methods that are now
a feature of conditioning have, of course, taken a long time
to build up. A survey of the leading features governing the
conditioning process has already been attempted, so that it
will suffice to emphasise now the fact that, in this respect,
an altogether new set of principles has had to be evolved, and
these have had a great effect upon the milling trade. As a
matter of fact, however, even in these cases, the underlying
principles which affect the grinding of the wheat have not
been greatly affected. The principles, however, governing
what may be termed the " inside commercial management "
of a mill—to coin an expression—have been completely
changed by increasing stress of modern competition and the
establishment of huge port mills making from 60/120 sacks
of flour an hour. In such cases an altogether new set of
economic principles has had to be evolved. The consideration
of the economics of a mill's management must now be left to
another occasion.

At the present time there are no signs of any changes in
the principles of milling. In the details, and what may be
termed the major details, however, many changes are being
made. One of the features of the milling engineering trade
has been the number of special patent and more or less secret
processes which have been put on the market. On the other
hand, the very fact that these experiments are being made
only serves to emphasise the fact that the main outlines of
the milling system have become stereotyped—or rather are so
considered. And thus while the tendency of the present time
is to leave the principles of milling alone, in regard to the
details a period of transformation and experiment is being
witnessed.

THE BREAK SYSTEM.

THE MODERN FLOUR ROLLER MILL.

Millers have always recognised the importance of the part which the break system plays in their mills. "Good breaking means good milling." Ever since the time when gradual reduction was first introduced into mills, the problem to which millers have given most attention is that of breaking the endosperm away from the bran. This done satisfactorily, good work in all the other departments of the mill is made possible, but where the breaking is badly done, either by reason of an inefficient system, or through the inefficient handling of a good system, then all the potentialities for high-class work in the other sections of the mill are hampered, and in some cases destroyed. The reason for this is not far to seek. The skin of wheat—the bran—is tough and considerable disintegrating force must be applied before it will break down and release the flour and middlings. But besides being tough, it is more or less brittle, is easily cut into shreds or powder, and thus apt to discolour anything with which it comes into contact—in this case the other products of the grind. The problem therefore the milling engineer and miller are set is to devise a method of breaking down the berry, so that it may be possible, in subsequent operations, to obtain the maximum yield of flour and broad, clean bran, and the minimum of bran powder and dust liable to spoil the flour.

Ever since gradual reduction established its supremacy, breaking has been usually accomplished by passing the wheat berry through a succession of pairs of grooved rolls. Notwithstanding this, there were for a number of years several alternative systems. For a time millstones were used to break down the wheat, rolls only being employed to reduce the middlings. This arrangement did not last for long, and experiments were made with a number of other grinding machines before grooved rolls were universally adopted to break down the grain. Some of these exhibited great peculiarities of design and may be described as the " freak " creations of the trade. The majority of them were never anything more than unsuccessful experiments and their trial resulted in loss of money both to the makers and the users of them. Others, however, for a time had quite an extended vogue among millers. Of these the most notable were the high speed disc machines. Some of these, in skilled hands, yielded quite excellent results as breaks, and a few of them were to be seen in use—as second and third breaks—in isolated mills in different parts of the country until a few years ago. But the discs had a number of defects which prevented them even having a chance of becoming really popular with millers. Even when they were doing good work, they took up more power than did rolls, they were apt to get out of order for no apparent reason, and a great deal of skill was required in adjusting them, while the cutting edges soon got blunt and required renewing. Their high speed and small capacity were other drawbacks. Thus practically in every respect the discs compared unfavourably with the work of the rolls, which had the inestimable advantage of being " Monday morning to Saturday night machines." At the same time, as the most serious competitors to the rolls as breaking machines they are worthy of mention.

Since discs were discarded, the roller mill has held undisturbed sway both for the breaks and the reductions. It may, therefore, be well, before proceeding to a detailed study of the practice of a modern four break system, briefly to consider the main points in the construction of a modern roller mill. As a matter of fact, roller mills are considerably older than many people imagine, for we have accounts of experiments with isolated rolls, or rollers as they were then termed, for grinding, or rather crushing, as far back as the eighteenth century. But it was not until their adoption in the mills of Buda Pesth that rolls became a commercial machine. The rolls did not come to England until they had become a proved commercial success. The first rolls were of the vertical type, one pair in a frame. Shortly afterwards the four-roller mill— two pairs on either side of one frame—was introduced, and, at about the same time, the three-high roll. This latter machine, which still may be seen in a few mills, had a wonderful vogue for a time. There is no doubt that the conception, or idea, of the machine is most brilliant, and in theory, economical, both of power and space. In practice, however, two great drawbacks combined to compel millers to abandon this type of roll. In the first place, the cross and channel feeds were never entirely satisfactory and often an absolute nuisance, in the second place, after a little time, the varied stresses set up by the peculiar pressures engendered by the rolls and the double grind, made it difficult to keep the rolls to their work, or, for long to maintain the adjustments. Shortly after the three-high mill, came the horizontal four-roller mill and the three types of machines were all to be seen for some years. The three-high mill, however, gradually dropped out, and the vertical and horizontal machines continued to compete for public favour. The balance of opinion came to be decidedly in favour of the vertical type, and this was the most generally installed until the modern diagonal roll was invented and superseded both the older types. At the present time though there are numbers of rolls of each kind running to-day, the diagonal mill is the pattern upon which all the English milling engineers make their rolls. On the Continent, however, the vertical mill is manufactured, while American millers still prefer horizontal machines.

The points of difference between the three types are worth a little consideration. The horizontal rolls have an advantage in that they are easy to feed, while the weight of the rolls does not come into play when making the adjustments. The rolls take up a large amount of floor space, but their chief drawback lies in the fact that they are least suited to be made in the large sizes preferred in this country, or to do the heavy continuous work that is expected here. In America all the milling machinery is of a lighter character, and this probably explains their popularity in that country. The grind is rather difficult of access, while when heavy pressure is being applied, all the pressure is supplied and borne by the adjustments.

The vertical rolls show to much greater advantage where constant, heavy work is required. Their adjustment is not so liable to vary and they are easier to keep down to their work. In the matter of floor space they are the most economical of all the different kinds of roller mill. The examination of the grinds is easy, but the necessity for a back plate and the impossibility of watching the feed into the nip of the rolls render the vertical mill the most difficult of any of the three types to feed quite accurately.

But both the two former types, as far as English engineers are concerned, have been almost abandoned in favour of the diagonal roll, which is now the pattern most largely manufactured in this country. The angle at which the rolls are set in the frame (about 45 degrees) makes this mill easier to feed than either of the two other types, while the examination of the grind is perfectly easy. The stock can be delivered over a feed roll into the nip of the roll at its natural angle of projection, and can be watched all the way. The fact, too, that the rolls are set at an angle makes it easier to obtain a fine adjustment. In addition, the rolls are made so perfectly that they keep well to their work, do not vibrate, grind evenly and keep cool. Altogether it cannot be doubted that the modern diagonal roller mill is a great advance upon all the previous types, although some very fine work may be done with the best types of vertical rolls.

The mills of late years have been made in an increasingly solid manner and regard above everything has been paid to the rigidity of the frame, so that vibration may be reduced to a minimum, and the rolls adapted for heavy work. The tendency has been towards the increasing use of longer and heavier mills. The standard sizes used in the smaller mills are 20 in. x 9 in., 24 in. x 9 or 10 in., 32 in. x 10 in., and in the larger mills 40 in. x 10 in. and 60 in. x 10 in., the latter size only being used as break rolls. In some mills the larger rolls are as much as thirteen inches in diameter.

It should be remembered, when considering the modern mill, that very many improvements have been made in the last few years, especially in the accessory fittings of the rolls. That is to say, the feeding devices, the adjustment apparatus, the bearings, the scrapers, and the like have all been made the subject of specialised attention, while finally engineers have vied with one another in producing the most handsome machine.

The bearings are usually made of phosphor bronze, they must be of ample length and diameter to withstand the great pressure that is put upon the rolls and spindles during grinding, without heating, and with a minimum of friction. In such circumstances the lubricating appliances are necessarily very important. All the makers of high class rolls provide automatic self-oiling bearings, so that a constantly circulating stream of oil may reach every part of the surface of the bearing.

The recognised material for the rolls is chilled iron. The chill is obtained by pouring the molten metal into a cold iron mould. The molten metal coming into contact with the cold iron of the mould is made to cool very quickly—is in fact " chilled " and thus it crystallises on the outside, while the inside cools at a more natural rate. As a result the surface of the roll, which is then turned true in a lathe, is very hard and peculiarly adapted to resist the great frictional stresses set up by the continual grinding. The core of the roll, on the other hand, though softer, is tough and well able to maintain the rigidity and toughness and the resistance to any tendency to spring or crack under shock that is so necessary in a heavy roller mill.

For reduction purposes rolls of other than chilled iron have been, and still are, used. Very early in the history of roller milling Wegmann brought out his porcelain rolls for use on the higher reductions. These met with great favour among millers and accomplished good work, but the earlier rolls were apt to crack, while under the stress of hard continual work they rapidly wore unevenly, and as a result millers in this country gave up using them. Later types of porcelain rolls have exhibited many improvements over the original makes and at the present time these rolls are used for reducing pure stocks at the head of the mill in many Continental and some English mills. In this country, however, they are only just recovering from the unpopularity which was occasioned by the defects mentioned above.

Very recently rolls have been introduced for reduction purposes made of a hard, reinforced, patent composition of various degrees of fineness of surface. The surface of the roll is very hard and any tendency to crack is obviated by the metallic reinforcement, which is quite a unique feature of these rolls. This is not the place to discuss their action, but it may be mentioned that these rolls have not yet had time to prove their quality. It has been necessary for the sake of completeness to refer to these various materials which are used in the manufacture of rolls, but it must be distinctly understood that in an altogether overwhelming majority of cases, even for reduction rolls, chilled iron is the material employed, while for the breaks it is universal.

The adjustment apparatus is probably the most important of what may be termed the accessories of the roller mill. In the first place there is the arrangement for putting the rolls in and out of gear. It is necessary that this arrangement should be simple and strong and quite rigid. In the modern diagonal roller mill the lower roll is the adjustable one. The bearing at each end is built on an arm, one end of which is hung on to the tension rod in connection with the compression spring, and the other end is pivoted on a fulcrum pin. The tension rods can be raised or lowered by means of handwheels, which work in connection with a nut and thread that carry the rod. In this way the rolls can be adjusted at either end. By depressing the throw-out lever an eccentric cam is operated at each end of the rolls and this lowers the adjusting mechanism, the tension rod and the roll, all together, and thus a clearance between the rolls, which need not be great, is effected.

In addition to the ordinary adjusting wheel there is, in practically every roller mill, a micrometer apparatus, made on the same principle as the vernier scale of a barometer, by this means an exceedingly delicate adjustment of the rolls is possible.

In addition, the throw-out lever always works in conjunction with the feed rolls, so that the latter are automatically stopped directly the rolls are put out of gear.

It should be noted that the adjustable rolls are carried on the compression levers, the top ones being fixed. Springs are necessary for two or three reasons. In the first place, the springs help to keep the rolls to their work, while in addition, if any hard foreign substance by any mischance gets between the rolls, the springs are compressed and allow it to pass through, at the same time taking up some of the great shock that occurs which otherwise might seriously damage the rolls. The springs also help to absorb any vibration which may be caused by the grinding action of the rolls.

Not less important than the adjustments are the feeding devices. In the days of the early roller mills these were often very crude and imperfect, but at the present time the feeding apparatus has been brought to a great pitch of perfection by the milling engineers. When designing the feeding gear of a roller mill regard must be paid to a number of considerations. In the first place the characteristics of the different stocks that are to be found in a mill vary from the whole grain to the fine '' woolly '' stock found in the last reduction feeds. Again, the feeding apparatus must be so constructed that, whether the roll be fully or barely fed, it may be possible to obtain an even line of feed right across it. At the present time the twin roller feed with an adjustable feed gate is often employed. For the breaks the feed rolls are usually grooved coarse, while in the case of the reductions a fairly finely fluted feed roll often delivers the stock over a polished feed plate from whence another fast running, finely threaded roll projects the material into the nip of the roll. The feed gate can usually be either set in a fixed position, or adjusted by means of automatically working springs, or the pitch and balance of the gate may be altered by means of screws. In addition to this there is generally another lever by which the whole feed gate may be lifted right up off the feed roll, in the event of any obstruction blocking the feed.

It may be convenient here to devote a few lines to the gearing, differential speeds, and the fluting of a modern roller mill. In the first place, the reason for the adoption of a differential may be mentioned. If there were no differential a single bruising or squeezing pressure would be all that it would be possible to obtain by means of rolls. In that case the material being ground would be flattened. With equal circumferential speeds there would be a limited release of middlings and it would be impossible to clean bran. When it came to reducing middlings they would be flaked into cakes and although some flour would be made it would require great pressure, and a large amount of power would be consumed practically to no purpose. The substitution of the principle of differential for that of simple pressure at once introduces another element into the grinding operations. A shearing, free-cutting action takes the place of a dull squashing squeeze. As a result the endosperm not only is liberated from the bran, but the product of the grind, as it has been cut and sheared, and not flattened and bruised, falls apart and can be the more easily treated in subsequent operations. The free cutting action is of course more apparent in the case of breaks than in that of reductions. The grooving that is employed to give the free cutting action mentioned also demands some attention. In the early days of roller milling there were many controversies as to what type of fluting gave the best results. Finally, however, the "sawtooth" pattern displaced all others. In this type the grooves are made chiselwise and the fast roll has the cutting edges facing in the direction of rotation, while the slow roll is grooved in exactly the opposite way. In this way the slow roll tends to hold the grain of wheat, or part of it, while the fast roll, rushing by, shears off a portion. The process is continued all through the break system. In order further to assist the shearing action, and also to prevent any possibility of the rolls interlocking, the flutes are not cut parallel to the axis of the roll but at an angle. This is termed the " spiral " and the result is that the edges of the flutes cross one another scissors fashion. The angle of the spiral varies somewhat, but is usually about 15 degs. or a deflection of one in seven The spiral very considerably assists the shearing action of the rolls and promotes a freer release of stock.

The differential speed between the fast and slow rolls is generally produced in this country by unequal gearing, though one firm of engineers makes rolls of unequal diameters with equal speeds. In America, however, the differential is sometimes obtained by two belts driving directly on to the respective rolls. This method, however, is not considered satisfactory by European engineers and either helical or cut gears, working in an oil bath, enclosed in a grease and oil tight gear case, are employed. The oil bath renders the gears, which are now very economical of power, almost noiseless.

Finally the drive from the mill shafting is by belt, that is to say for a four roller mill there is one belt drive to each pair of rolls. Here again the American and European methods differ, as in America both pairs of rolls are often driven by a single belt kept tight by a jockey pulley. This method of driving, too, has long been superseded in this country, as the jockey pulley absorbs a good deal of power and the alternating strains put upon the belts tend to wear them out very quickly.

Such is an outline of the main features of a modern flour roller mill.

THE BREAK SYSTEM.

THE IMPORTANCE OF THE ROLLERMAN.

Having given a brief sketch of the character of the principal machine in a modern flour mill, viz., the four roller mill, it will be well now to consider what are the chief characteristics of a modern break system, and to discuss the principles underlying its successful working, also a few of its many possibilities and peculiarities. But before in any way dealing with the details of the system there are still a few preliminary points which call for a little notice. In the first place, a word seems necessary as to the responsibilities of the break rollerman in a flour mill. To become a roller-man is, or should be, the ambition of every operative who enters a mill; in passing, it can be noted that to have the necessary skill to become one is a necessity for the young master miller who intends to become expert in his art. But the young operative has several positions to fill before he becomes a " miller." On the centrifugal floor he will gain a general knowledge of the mill's working, and a specialised acquaintance with the " chokes " that sometimes occur in the best of mills; but more important he will, or should, get into an early habit of making careful and regular tests of the work of the machines under his control, and this habit, once acquired, will stand him in good stead when he attains to a position of responsibility. On the purifier floor he will see how skill affects the working of machines, and he will see, too, how soon neglect of attention will show itself later in the system and bring the reduction rollerman upstairs to call him to account. But it will be when he gets down on the roller floor that he will be able to realise how much the work of the mill depends upon the operative in charge of the rolls, and this leads to a consideration of the possibilities of the break system. Where there are two rollermen the head rollerman is the breaksman, for with hardly any exaggeration it can be said that the break rollerman holds in his hand almost all—at any rate a very great many—of the potentialities the mill possesses. Putting the matter in another way, he certainly can, by only a comparatively small neglect of his duties, turn upside down the good work of the mill and turn a comfortable profit into a bad loss. The nature of the feed to the reductions, the release of semolina and middlings, the amount of stock going to the head of the mill, the quality of the bran, the clean up, the amount and quality of break flour made, the presence or absence of bran powder, all these things depend to a great extent upon the setting of the breaks, and on them depends the quality of the mill's work. It is therefore clearly not necessary to labour the point about the importance of the break system or the responsibility of the rollerman. It is, and will be, presumed in this connection that well cleaned and conditioned wheat is arriving at the first break. Without that the best mill cannot be made to produce good results.

There have, of course, been changes both in the systems and methods of breaking, though more in the latter than the former. To the systems in which machines other than grooved rolls were used, reference has been made already. In addition it may be mentioned that besides their mechanical shortcomings, very often, in fact usually, their work, judged by modern standards, failed for one of two reasons. Usually *either* they cut the bran up badly (thus also making bran powder) while effecting a large release of good semolina and middlings, or *else* in making broad clean bran an excessive quantity of break flour was also made with comparatively very few good middlings. It was thus left for time to prove that a succession of pairs of grooved rolls was the best apparatus for breaking down the berry and securing at the same time both the maximum of good stock to the head of the mill (thus ensuring a length of patents) and also broad clean bran. The causes of the decline of the other systems, and of the stones, have been traced in some detail, so that the *reason* for our mills being constructed as they are at present may be brought out. From this a further question is suggested; what does the rollerman reckon to accomplish when he adjusts, or " sets " his breaks? Briefly, it may be said that he aims at first turning the berry, as it were, inside out, and then in successive stages shearing off the endosperm a portion at a time without cutting the bran, finally leaving it (the bran) clean. In doing this he reckons to make a maximum amount of semolina and larger middlings, only a small quantity of break flour, and to leave the bran quite clean and broad and to make a minimum of bran powder. Such is an outline of the main ideas and principles governing the handling of the breaks. None of the foregoing aims must be accomplished at the expense of the others, and this is where the operative's skill is taxed. It is comparatively easy to accomplish some of the aims mentioned, but to accomplish them all at once requires a true miller's skill.

There have, too, been considerable changes in the practice of working the breaks, that is to say the relative importance and the work assigned to the separate breaks have altered, but these differences of practice have been occasioned by the continually shifting ideas respecting the proper condition of wheat, to which reference has continually to be made. Before all foreign wheats were washed the rollerman had quite a different product coming on to his first break from what he has to-day, or had, say, twenty years ago when some foreign wheats were washed and not others. It follows that different methods in regard to breaking have had to be found. The improvement, too, in dry cleaning—particularly seed extracting—has also helped to render the rollerman's task more simple. Yet at the same time neither the theory nor the principles, nor indeed the aims of the rollerman have changed during the whole of the period.

At the present time in the U.K. the four break system is adopted in an overwhelming majority of mills. A few mills can be found which have five breaks; there are quite a number of small, and one or two large mills, in which there are but three, but speaking generally it may be said that four is the accepted number of breaks in this country, nor is there any evidence to show—except when special circumstances have to be met—that any departure is likely to be made from it. On the Continent there are often longer break systems. In Hungary six is by no means an uncommon number, and in France five may be said to be the usual number. With regard to the two latter countries, it is well to note that in the case of the former refinement and elaboration of system have from the first been practised, while French mills, whether inland or near a port, practically always grind principally French wheat, which, being tough, soft and thick-skinned, is precisely the kind on which a long break system may be employed to the best advantage. In this country all numbers of breaks have been tried from two to eight, but the big numbers were early found to be excessive, while on a three break system it was found that results suffered from the drastic treatment that had to be meted out at each stage. This necessitated a large quantity of break flour, and in addition it was found rather difficult to make a finish and broad bran at the same time, while the fine side of the last break, whence a lot of rather gritty stock often came, gave much trouble. And so, though for mills making chiefly a straight run flour the three break system was often installed, five breaks came to be used in large mills and four in medium sized ones. This number has since been reduced by one, and the four break system now reigns in England. The general change from five breaks to four may probably be ascribed partly to a desire on the part of millers to have their systems as simple as was consistent with efficiency, and partly to the fact that the tougher nature of the wheat coming on to the first break did away with the necessity for an excessively gentle first break and so allowed the system to be shortened. References continually have to be made to the effect of conditioning upon the break system, the former has such an influence upon the latter. The general adoption, too, of the principle that the moisture content of the wheat is a matter to be determined by the miller and not by Nature, has had considerable indirect influence upon many matters connected with milling. In some cases the connection is not at first apparent. Thus the attitude of mind and the spirit of enquiry prompted by the results of experiments in conditioning has probably—the suggestion is put tentatively—had some effect upon and hastened the modern developments of flour treatment and improving. The principle of improving the natural properties of the wheat by carefully calculated methods is the same whether water be added to the grain to bring it into the best milling condition, or whether the flour or mill stocks are sprayed to better the flour, or whether pure soluble phosphates or persulphates be added in order that better, lighter, and therefore more wholesome bread may be obtained from the flour after it has been milled. The means employed are different, but the principle is the same. But this has been by way of parenthesis, and in explanation of the remark that the effect of modern methods of conditioning has been very much to alter the methods and practices of the break rollerman.

THE BREAK SYSTEM.

THE FIRST BREAK.

Thus, when it was found that with well conditioned wheat there was no need for•extra tenderness at the first break and the first break began to take its place with others in regard to the amount of work performed by it, the number of breaks was reduced from five to four, and here, again, perhaps, somewhat in parenthesis, but yet with a direct bearing upon the mill system generally, it may be said that it cannot be regarded as anything but an advantage to the miller, when his system is made more simple. The shorter break system meant less machinery, less space, less power and less capital expense, and in the case under notice the efficiency of the mill was not at all affected and improved. Simplicity and efficiency often go together in a mill system. Of course, it is not suggested that efficiency in any way should be sacrificed in order that a miller may boast how simple his system is, and a careful distinction must be drawn between a simple straightforward system and a " short " system. The two things are different. Everyone agrees that a mill system should be as straightforward as possible, but there have been and doubtless will be systems which should give perfect results, but which fail in the practical test of every day working by reason of their complication. It may not be out of place to emphasise here the necessity for having a mill system which, though it may have any amount of refinement shall yet in its essential points be straightforward, and because straightforward the easier to keep working at a high standard of efficiency from one week to another.

Perhaps it will be simpler if instead of discussing the breaks generally they are first of all considered separately and in order, and then at the end a few general remarks made about the whole system. With regard to what may be termed the practice of milling at this stage it is well to state at once some divergence of opinion exists among millers as to how exactly the rolls should be set at the several stages. This is only to be expected. In any case, however, where any definite statement is made with regard to any point which may be disputed or doubtful, the attempt has been made to give what may be termed modern orthodox practice.

The first break therefore claims attention. Apart from its priority it is perhaps the most important, certainly one of the most interesting, of all the machines in the mill. But it has not ever been thus, and in the early days of roller milling it was regarded rather as a necessary evil whose operations should be got over as lightly and quickly as possible, rather than as the most efficient instrument in the mill for making the best semolina. The question naturally arises as to why this change has taken place. Once more it has to be said that the difference between the work done on the first break now and twenty-five years ago is due to the altered methods of treating the wheat mixture. Two of the bugbears of the early millers were " crease dirt " and " blue flour." Neither of those things are ever mentioned now, but they were very real troubles to the first roller millers, and no end of time and money was spent in endeavouring to banish them from the mill. It was found that the flour from the first break was the worst in the mill, and to account for this the existence of dirt locked away in the crease of the wheat was postulated. Whatever the cause, it was agreed that there was something inherently wrong with first break flour, and consequently millers determined to have as little of it as possible. As a result the first break in many mills was treated almost as a final cleaning machine. Of course, we know now that crease dirt was conquered by the advent of the washer, and that if " blue " flour occurs it means that the brushes and exhausts have been neglected. But at that time it was not so. The fact remains also that, apart from the little dirt that inevitably escapes the dry cleaning machines, wheat until properly conditioned is not in a state to stand severe treatment on the first break. Consider the position of affairs. If Indians are the only wheats regularly to be washed, the mixture is bound to come on to the first break dry and brittle, and the bran " short " and very liable both to chip and powder. The effect of a heavy first break— as the word " heavy " in this connection is now understood —on such a mixture must be to cut up the bran so as to affect its sale; the break flour would be greatly damaged by the bran powder. The release of semolina and middlings would be good, but the purifier feeds would contain so many impurities that these latter machines would probably be unable to lift them all out while rather impure scratch stock might be looked for in excessive quantities. In addition the stock at the latter breaks would never recover from its early gruelling. Thus, it can be seen that on a dry mixture a severe treatment at the first break is out of the question if the best work is to be accomplished. Assume, however, that all the mixture except the English has been washed and another aspect is immediately put upon the question. The addition of moisture toughens the bran, mellows the endosperm, does away with the tendency to " fly " and " chip " under treatment, allows the semolina to be released easily, and in fact the rollerman has almost another product coming to his first break : at any rate in the early stages quite different treatment is needed. As a matter of fact the mixture has slowly increased in the matter of its moisture content during the last twenty years, even since the practice of washing all the foreign wheats was introduced. At the beginning of that period the mixture was principally unwashed. A dozen years ago the moisture content was quite considerably less than is now generally the case. The increasing additions of moisture continued and though there has been perhaps a slight reaction from the heavy conditioning that was practised a couple of years ago, still at the present time perhaps between 16.5 and 17.5 is the accepted percentage of moisture for those mills which do not add moisture to the mill products during the process of milling. And while the moisture content has been increasing so has the work done by the first break been increased. It is recognised that only on the first and second breaks, where the flutes are coarse, can the best semolina be obtained and consequently if little work be done in the first break a chance has been lost of getting a big percentage of high class stock to the head of the mill. And so in most modern mills the half split berry is no longer seen, and instead the rollerman set their rolls to obtain, some 25 per cent., and some as much as 30 per cent., of release of break chop right at the start of the system. The condition of the wheat prevents the bran from being cut up and also ensures that the semolina and scratch stocks shall not be laden with impurities. The principle of the necessity of getting a good release of semolina and middlings is so generally accepted that there are several special first break machines designed with this object in view. With regard to the amount of chop stock actually made, with ordinary grooved rolls in good condition up to 30 per cent. release may be obtained if the rolls are handled with good judgment and the condition of the mixture is right.

The adjustment of the first break should not present any great difficulties. The chief point is to know when to leave off bringing the rolls up together. In order to aid him in this, and in order to be assured that he is getting about a normal and proper release, the rollerman usually provides himself with sieves and scales so that he may the better keep a constant stream of feed to his purifiers, and also so that he may compare the work of one day with another. These sieves and scales may be made extremely useful accessories to the rollerman provided he uses them intelligently and does not let them fetter his better judgment or make an automaton of him, for if they do the last state of the breaks may easily become worse than the first. The rollerman, in one sense, is not the arbiter of his own fortunes, for he has to get the best result he can out of the wheat in spite of the fact that no human skill can prevent some variation in the condition of the mixture. Thus, to take a concrete illustration, it does not follow that because 30 per cent. of release is being satisfactorily effected on a Saturday, that 27 per cent. release on a Monday morning, when the wheat is in a different condition, may not cause everything to be far too much chopped up. All these little things someone has to bear in mind or else there is trouble. As a matter of fact above the 30 per cent. limit it is not generally found desirable to go, though there are some millers who like to get 33 per cent. at this stage. This, however, means rather severe treatment and a tendency for the percentage of break flour to increase out of proportion to the extra release, while the bran may also be found to be rather small. So much for the first break.

THE BREAK SYSTEM.

INCREASES IN SURFACE.

THE IMPORTANCE OF SHARP FLUTING.

The second break has always been regarded as the break for work. In this respect there has been no deviation in practice right from the earliest period of roller milling until the present time. The stock, immediately after the preliminary breaking, is in a condition such that it will be less susceptible to severe treatment than at any other stage of the system. The rollerman therefore naturally seizes his chance. The wheat, after passing the first break, is opened out, and the second break rolls can be set to shear away the major portion of the endosperm adhering to the bran. This latter being tough suffers no hurt, while if the wheat has been properly conditioned there will be a large quantity of the very best middlings and semolina made. The break flour here is better than anywhere else in the break system. Work neglected at this stage means that the two latter breaks, instead of having only to release the rest of the poorer middlings and to clean the bran, have to do the work the previous rolls have left undone, and this makes a finish doubtful and difficult. The general consensus of opinion among operatives goes to show that the setting of the second break rolls presents fewer difficulties than either of the others. Besides, the essentials of all roll setting—keeping the rolls parallel and attention to feeds and so forth—and the knowledge of when enough work has been done, there are no special diffi culties likely to be encountered at this break.

The third break has diminished in importance very much in the same proportion as the first break has risen. As a

102

result, at the present time its work is confined to shearing off the last of the good middlings from the broader bran and getting the smaller stock in a condition so that not too much is left for the final pair of rolls. If, however, the first break is not making a sufficient release of stock, though some of the deficiency may be recovered on the second, of necessity the third break has more to do.

It is, of course, the custom to divide the breaks into " fine " and " coarse " sides. The broad bran goes on the one side and the small, " short " hard stock goes to the other. Without exaggeration it may be said that the fine break stock gives the rollerman twice as much trouble as the coarse. It is about equally easy to make the mistake both of doing too much and too little. In the first case he will tend to cut the stock up to powder, which will mean small bran and ragged semolina; in the latter case the chance of getting stock to the purifiers will have been lost, and on the last break the problem will be again presented in an aggravated form, with the additional feature that either he must risk hard sharps or else he must grind everything up, in doing which he will make bad break flour and poor middlings. The middlings, in any case from the third break, will be fewer and smaller than those from the earlier breaks; the flour, too, from this break will not be quite so good as that from the second, the reason for this is not quite apparent, but in all probability it is because the end of the system is being approached and consequently there are more chances of contamination from bran powder.

The last break, whether it be the fourth or any other, is always, and has always been, the operatives' bugbear. On this break the rollerman has to shave off—the word fairly accurately describes the operation—any particles of flour that the previous breaks have left. This is difficult enough, but in doing this the line has to be drawn so that the bran is not injured. This is where troubles begin. The bran can easily be damaged, and easier still bran powder can be made that will irreparably damage the bran flour and in addition be a further nuisance, as it will in slight degree mix with other stocks to their hurt. Then, too, the fact that the rolls work so very close together—the two rolls are not more than 1/300th part of an inch apart—makes it at the same time both difficult but absolutely essential to maintain them exactly parallel.

When finally finished, the best bran is thin, light, broad and neither curled nor dusty, while the marks of the corrugations of the last break can often faintly be traced. As a matter of fact, the quality of the finished bran is a fairly reliable indication of the work of the break system as a whole.

The characteristic points about the four breaks having thus been summed up, there remain two or three general observations to be made. First, with regard to the fluting and differential. The need for a differential and fluting, and the style and pattern of the grooves, have already been discussed. The actual differential usually employed in England to-day for the breaks is $2\frac{1}{2}$ to 1. There is, of course, no *a priori* reason why all the breaks should have the same fixed differential, indeed as far as can be seen, reasoning would seem to show that the differential should be changed for different stocks. For instance, it seems right that the shearing action of the breaks should be increased for the last break, and the grinding action increased for the second. And this was the plan adopted at one time. Recently, however, the $2\frac{1}{2}$ to 1 differential has come into general favour. Nevertheless there are a number of millers who use the higher differential for the last break and who assert that better work can thereby be done. It may be recalled that the higher differentials in certain cases are extensively used in America, while in this country until a few years ago 3 to 1 was the accepted differential both for scratch stock and for the last break.

As to the fluting, the actual number of grooves employed at the several breaks has never been constant. All that can be said is that in the majority of systems 28 grooves to the inch has been about the limit in one direction and 8 or 10 grooves per inch in the other. The 8 and 10 fluting for the first break lasted a very long time, but like nearly everything else in connection with that machine it has changed with altered circumstances, and now (except for special machines) the general standard adopted for a new mill is 12 flutes to the inch. This fluting is found to give better results than the old, when the hard work on the first break is attempted, while the smaller number is better when a half cracked berry is desired. For the other breaks 14-16 grooves for the second, 18-22 for the third and 26-28 grooves to the inch for the fourth may be taken as including the average limits of modern practice. It should be said that some firms have a special first break fluting designed to give a specially big release. In this case they groove the fast and slow rolls differently, the slow or holding roll being grooved 15-16 to the inch, while the first roll is fluted 5 or 6 to the inch.

A consideration of the break system cannot be left without some reference to the necessity for sharp flutes. Dull breaks, if all the machines are allowed to get really bad and neglected, will produce a very fair imitation of chaos in a mill. This is even more the case than ever before now that the mixture is milled in its tough condition. Take a case where the break rolls have been allowed to become really dull—an extreme case for the purpose of illustrating the point. What will be the results? In the first place, the semolina and middlings will be about equally reduced in quantity, size and quality. The semolina will tend to be ill-shaped and ragged because the offal will have been torn, not cut, by the blunt edges of the flutes, and for the same reason other powdery impurities will also be present in large quantities. Then the bran will be small, but not on that account clean. On the contrary, it is likely to be dusty and thick, and any attempt to make a real clean up on the last two breaks is only likely to accentuate the evils already present and to make still smaller bran, still more powder and still worse bran flour. It can thus be seen that in this extreme case of all the flutes being dull together, the whole flow of the mill would become disorganised. The only stock that will seem improved will he the break flour from the first three breaks. This will be greatly increased in quantity and will look better than usual, as indeed it should, seeing that it will contain a good percentage of flour that ordinarily goes to the patent sack via the A., B. or C. rolls. Of course, in an ordinary way not all these effects will be observed from dull rolls. An exaggerated illustration has been taken purposely in order that the tendencies may be the better illustrated. In general, fluted rolls give the best results about two or three months after they are put in; then for some time the work is about even, and then it gradually declines. The life of a roll varies greatly according to the work it is doing, the way it is handled and a number of circumstances, so that definite statements on the point are not much use.

A word must be inserted with reference to the amount of roll surface necessary for the breaks. Time was when 30 inches per sack per hour capacity of a mill was thought enough, and 35 inches ample, surface. The changing mixture, however, aided very greatly by the more or less general use of some form or another of pneumatic scalping, which presupposed these feeds for the air currents to play upon, made an extended surface necessary. To-day 45 inches per sack for a new mill may be called the standard, but mills are put up with break surfaces varying from 40 inches to nearly 50 inches per hourly sack capacity. This extension of surface must be regarded an improvement, both in theory and practice. The whole underlying idea in the break system is that the berry and the half-broken down stock shall be subjected to the free cutting action of the flutes. If the rolls are fed too heavily then the disintegrating force is applied, not by the flutes, but by the berries of portions of stock rubbing against one another. This bruising, squashing action is the very thing the miller wants to avoid, and its effects can only be to damage the break stock and to make attrition flour. Then, too, in any system in which air currents or other devices make separations in the roll hopper, these feeds are practically a necessity. In this connection it is well to remember that the extra surface demands that great care shall be taken with the feeding, and the rollerman's task of seeing that the various rolls are evenly fed the whole length of the rolls is made more **difficult.**

106

It has been said that the standard length of break surface lies round about 45 per sack. In the ordinary way the surface is not distributed evenly between the four breaks. The second often has more surface allotted to it than either of the other breaks, and in any case shares with the third more surface than the first or fourth. However, different millers and milling engineers have different views, and the length of surface at any particular break depends considerably upon the system employed.

In concluson, it may be noted that no word has been said about the rollerman's mechanical equipment, his knowledge of his machines, his care of them, the necessity for keeping the feeds even, and the rolls parallel and the like. It need not be said how important are these matters, or how much they mean to the good working of the breaks. But this very importance prevents their being treated at the end of a long article on the break system, and the mention of them—so that it may not be thought their value has been overlooked—must suffice for the present.

SCALPING AND GRADING.

VARIOUS SCALPERS.

The operation of sifting off the finished or partly-finished bran from the remainder of the products of the breaks has always been known as scalping. The origin of the term in connection with a distinctive operation in flour milling is wholly doubtful; it seems, however, quickly to have sprung into general usage, for no other term has ever been in competition with it. The necessity for scalping is obvious. No good work in a flour mill could be done if half reduced bran, semolina, middlings and flour were to be subjected, all together, to a series of grindings. The flour in such a case would be infinitely worse than that made on the stone system. Accordingly, as soon as the principle of gradual reduction was adopted some form of scalping after every operation was recognised as necessary. As a matter of fact, three separations are essential. The stock to go forward to the next break must first of all be separated from all the rest. Then the chop stock must be divided into (a) that which requires further treatment on the reduction or scratch rolls, and (b) flour. As a matter of fact, the term scalping can only be applied with strict accuracy to the first of these separations, the other two being "grading" and "dusting" respectively. The three operations, however, are closely related, are often performed on the same machine and may conveniently be treated together.

Until comparatively quite recently—within the last ten years or so—scalping had not quite the same detailed attention from milling engineers as the other departments of the mill. The breaks had received unremitting attention; purification was rightly deemed of extreme importance and had probably been the subject of more labour than any other

· 108

section of the mill. On the other side of the mill, methods of preparing and conditioning the wheat had been vastly improved. At the same time, break flour still remained one of the miller's troubles, though the general use of the washer had done much to improve it. But at length milling engineers began to turn their attention towards scalping with a view to improving the methods of treating the break stock. The result of their labours is the beautifully designed break systems that are seen to-day.

Before considering the various methods of scalping in detail, it may perhaps be well to inquire what are the essentials of good scalping and how it has been accomplished, so that the reason for the present systems may be the more apparent. In every case, both here and elsewhere, the attempt has been made, by an analysis of the causes which have led to the older methods of milling either to be maintained or superseded, to give a clear idea of the " why " and the "wherefore" of a modern mill system. Only by a knowledge of this "why" and "wherefore" is it possible to obtain a real grasp of the system.

Reference has been made to the quality of break flour. This from the first gave the roller millers trouble on account of the fact that it could never be reckoned on to improve any grade, while especially in the early times, with unskilful handling of the machines, it might seriously lessen the general quality of the flour made. In addition, the more there is of it, obviously the less can there be of other and better grades. The cause of the poor quality of the break flour for some time was in dispute. It is obvious that there can be nothing inherently wrong with it and the bad qualities must be attributed to some external cause. It is now apparent that the indifferent quality of first break flour in the early days was due largely to the fact that when the mixture was milled dry it was impossible to send wheat on to the first break quite free from dust. This, of course, sifted out with the flour made by the first break and naturally spoiled its quality. When the damper mixtures came the break flour was greatly improved, as not only was the presence of dust

109

obviatèd, but also the grist being tougher was not so liable to chip and to powder and thus contaminate the flour.

But although washing, by improving the grist, had done much to better the break flour it was felt that there was still room for improvement. But it became evident that the reason that break flour is often of poor quality must be found in the fact that flour becomes contaminated by other products of the break or in some other way. It so happens that flour has an amazing affinity for any kind of dirt and very little contact with such is required to injure it seriously. In addition, experience has also shown that attrition flour, that is to say flour made by semolina or middlings, being thrown about in spouts or elevators or through overmuch dressing surface, is the worst flour ever made in a mill. Finally, it can also be shown that inefficient scalping, that is to say, the sending on to the next roll of stock from which all the flour stock and middling have not been eliminated, means also bad, and very bad, work. For in the necessarily violent action of the breaks the flour and middlings will be squashed up with the bran and damaged in yet another way. From the above the essentials to good scalping may be deduced.

In the first place, it may be taken that efficiency must be secured. Then again, in order to lessen the risk of contamination, quickness or despatch in action is obviously an advantage in a scalper, and lastly so that attrition flour may not be made, gentleness in action is essential.

For some time centrifugals and reels were used as scalpers. The centrifugal has the advantage of being thorough in its action, quick also it is, but gentle it is not. The action is entirely the reverse and soon millers began to dislike the rough treatment which the stock was bound to receive in a centrifugal and which literally made attrition flour and mixed the break flour up with any little dust or bran powder there might be in the break product. Nor was the reel more satisfactory; its action was less violent, but it was more protracted and the machine, in addition, took more space than did the centrifugal. At the present time only seldom is centrifugal scalping installed right through a mill, but the centrifugal is usually retained to treat four-break stock where thorough efficiency in action is the one thing needful.

After the centrifugal and reel scalping had been found too severe, sieves, both reciprocating and rotary, were largely adopted as scalpers, and in many mills scalping is still performed by them. They were found to be distinctly an improvement upon the older types, particularly the centrifugal. They were gentler, the bran stock naturally rose to the top, the flour and heavier material sank to the bottom and sifted through, thus lessening the chance of contamination. They were efficient, provided there was a sufficiency of dressing surface, but in big plants took up a considerable amount of room and necessitated a good many accessory fittings. After sieves came plansifters, but in this country the use of these was abandoned for a time owing to mechanical difficulties. When these were finally overcome the plansifter was again installed, this time with success. Their action is admirably adapted for scalping, perhaps to a greater degree than in the case of sieves, as the large bran stock floats on the top and the flour and middlings, being smaller and heavier, naturally sink to the bottom and sift through beneath. In addition, the number of separations that can be made in one machine does away with the necessity for a large amount of spouting and elevating, and thus, in one plansifter, stock can be scalped and the throughs graded and dusted without any intermediate handling in elevators and spouts, and the stock is freed from many chances of contamination, and the manufacture of attrition flour. Altogether, it may be safely said that of the purely mechanical moving sifters the plansifter cannot be surpassed for scalping.

Yet after all the experiments that have been described neither millers nor engineers were quite satisfied and finally they employed a yet gentler separating medium than any that had been tried before, namely air currents. Several systems have been invented within a short time, and now full advantage is taken of the delicate separations that can be effected by properly regulated draughts in scalping. At the same time.

the modern systems all seek to eliminate the break flour and smallest middlings from the rest of the break product immediately upon its release before there can be any question of contamination. It can be seen how great an improvement this is upon even the best of the old systems. When the break chop has to be spouted down to the elevator boot, violently caught by the buckets, hoisted up and thrown with more or less force into the delivery spout whence it finally is delivered to the scalper, there is obviously bound to be a number of opportunities, both for the manufacture of attrition flour and the contamination of the break flour before the scalper is even reached. That this actually took place may be inferred from the improved results which the newer systems have been able to attain over the older ones, and particularly over those in which plansifters found no place.

SCALPING AND GRADING.

The name of pneumatic scalping was early given to the new style of scalping, and it is a very happy one. The pneumatic systems divide themselves into two divisions (*a*) those in which the chief separations are made solely by gravity and air currents, and (*b*) those in which air currents and bolters combine to effect the scalping.

Considering first the earliest, and perhaps the simplest in its governing idea, of the systems of pneumatic scalping, the separation is effected immediately under the nip of the rolls by merely placing an adjustable division board under the diagonal rolls in the hopper of the roller mill. It was found that by the help of this simple contrivance the stock naturally divides itself into two distinct portions by the action of the combined forces of momentum and gravity aided by air currents. As the stock leaves the nip of the rolls on the outer (door) side is found the heavy half-finished bran-stock and the semolina and larger middlings, while the flour, fine middlings and dunst fall more directly down on the other side of the division board.

In addition, an air current draws off light beeswing and pure offal, which is thus prevented from going right through the system. It can be seen that the main ideas' governing this method of scalping are very simple and there is practically nothing to get out of order. The exact position of the division board can be altered at will, as with radically different mixtures or conditions the throw of the stock will be affected, but the adjustment is not difficult to make. In the system under notice the semolina and bran stock are subsequently dealt with on spout scalpers and the flour dusted out of the middlings in ordinary way on a centrifugal.

It will be noticed that the requirements which were earlier stated to be essential for good scalping are taken into consideration, and the scalping of the stock is accomplished without the break flour ever coming into contact with that which might contaminate it, so it is separated from the rest of the break stock instantaneously on its release, while the danger of any of the middlings or half-finished stock being knocked about and attrition flour made is obviated by the gentleness of the operations.

The system very briefly described has been adopted in a number of mills, large and small. In the next under notice, also very widely favoured, the method of scalping is somewhat different. The whole of the break product is carried to a machine which is known as a cyclo-pneumatic separator. The break product is fed on to a revolving disc which spreads the stock into a thin spray of corelike shape. Whirling air draughts play upon the spray and draw upwards all the lighter middlings, dunst and flour. The broken wheat, semolina and heavy middlings fall through the air currents, which have freed them from dust. Both the aspirations and the heavy stock are then treated on plansifters and the usual separations made. In this system, too, the early separation of pure offal from the break products occupies a distinctive place and adds to the worth of the cyclo-pneumatic separator.

The conjunction, too, of the pneumatic principle and the thorough but gentle action of the flow-sifters on which all the secondary separations are made—the grading and dusting —has proved very successful. In this case also the whole scheme of the operations is simple, and this class of system also ranks as one of the leading scalping systems.

In yet other systems the scalping is effected in the roll hopper. The scheme of these is that immediately under the nip of the rolls is placed a sieve, while in some cases lower in the hopper is a second sieve. Both these sieves, where there are two, are stationary, or are vibrated slightly by means of automatic hammers or a cam. The action is as follows :—Immediately after leaving the nip of the rolls the break stock falls on to the first sieve clothed fine. Through this pass the flour and the finest middlings, assisted by air currents which greatly aid the separators. The flour is thus eliminated from the rest of the break product practically immediately on release. The bottom sieve takes out all the chop stock and tails over the bigger stock to be treated in the next break, quite scalped. In this method of scalping, too, the various breaks are often placed on different floors, the third break being on the roller floor (the fourth, as stated above, having as usual a centrifugal scalper), the second on a floor above, and the first on one above this. By this plan the unfinished break stock is sent from one break to another with the minimum of handling, spouts and elevators, and in this way the danger of making attrition flour or bran powder is greatly lessened. The throughs of the two sieves, *i.e.*, the fine chop and the coarser chop, are treated either on a plansifter or on sieves. The air currents, which assist the stock through the sieves in the roll hopper, are also utilised to exhaust away any light offal which may have been made In some systems which adopt this style of pneumatic scalping there is only one sieve under the roll hopper and this simplification of the system is favoured by a good number of millers. The only drawback to the system is to be found in the number of spouts which emanate from the roll hopper. Such, in the briefest outline, are the striking features of those systems of scalping whose main features differ widely from one another. It can be seen that the inventors of each have kept before them the main principles of scalping which were stated to be essentially important, and it would be invidious—even if it were possible—to single out either of these systems for special praise. In each case efficiency, celerity and gentleness in action, with the elimination of the pure offal as soon as made are secured.

The clothing adopted on scalpers perhaps calls for a brief notice. For the moment it is only necessary to be concerned with the clothing of the actual scalper—that is to say, with the number over which stock is sent to the next break. The clothing of the various graders and the rules that govern it can best be dealt with later. It is, as in most cases connected with milling, impossible to give fixed standards, but the general lines on which the clothing is regulated may be indicated. During the past few years there has been a tendency to clothe scalpers slightly more finely than formerly was the custom. Thus, while at one time it was common only to send on stock from the first break which could not go through No. 18 wire, to-day any stock that will not go through 20 or even 22 wire is sent on for treatment. Apart from this 20/22 after the first break, 22/24 after the second, 24/26 after the third and 34/38 after the fourth, on the scalpers may be regarded as about including the limits of modern practice, though actual numbers will vary somewhat according to the needs of the system, or the predilections of the miller or engineer who is responsible for the flow sheet.

It will be noticed that the numbers get finer as the breaks are reached. This needs a little qualification, for, as a matter of fact, in not a few mills the scalpers, after the first and second breaks are clothed the same, the reason being that at both breaks there is a good quantity of larger granular products. There is, of course, a reason for this practice of raising the wire numbers, as for every process in the flour mill. The underlying idea is that as the break stock proceeds down the system, particles of the same size get rather worse in quality. Thus, in order to make the point clearer, take the extreme cases of the first and last break. At the fourth break only a very little flour is left on the bran. As this is so any granular flour containing particles can be only small, while there will be a comparatively large amount of small bran or coarse sharps. Accordingly, the cover must be altered to suit the needs of the case. At the third break the same arrangement applies only in a considerably lesser degree, as here there is always some amount of granular stock, so that the cover of the third break scalper, though of a higher number than that of the first or second break scalpers, is not clothed up as is the bran scalper.

There is not much that can be said about the operatives' duties in connection with scalpers, for this department of the mill, being in its scheme and working comparatively simple, depends more than other sections of the mill upon the system rather than the operative; though, of course, very great care must be taken to see that the air draughts, in connection with the pneumatic system, are maintained constant. At the same time the operative will find that some work will be required from him to keep the plant up to concert pitch. Weather fluctuations may easily give him trouble, or if the mixture happens to be a little over damp, or both occur at the same time, a tendency to choke may be observed. Or more probably, he may find that the feed to the breaks is coming through dusty. He will know at once what is wrong. In such a case the only thing the miller can do is to brush by hand all the sieves which are accessible, or he might even have very slightly to ease his feed. At all times he will have to keep an eye on the covers of the scalpers and the work of the pneumatic machines. In other ways the operative will find that the scalping machines or apparatus will give him but little trouble, only requiring, in fact, the ordinarily careful attention which all moving machinery demands.

PURIFIERS AND PURIFICATION.

The purifier dates back to that time when rolls were nearly unknown, and high grinding was only just being thought of by the generality of millers. The first purifiers were brought out in Hungary, France and the United States about, or a little previous to, 1870. Some primitive machines had probably been made before that time, but the practical history of the purifier may be said to have commenced with the inventors Cabane, Lacroix, Whitmore, Hunter, Smith, and others.

Apart from offal sorters and the like machines, it was the first machine which neither bolted flour nor had anything to do with the grinding, and so it was the forerunner of the big array of machines which grade and purify and generally perform what may be termed the intermediate separators between the scalpers and the smooth rolls.

Various authorities, however, do not quite agree as to who was the actual inventor or what the first machine, but the point is immaterial. The purifier has another distinction connected with its introduction. Not only did its invention give an immense fillip to the practice of high grinding and gradual reduction, which was then coming into prominence, but it also became the incidental herald of an agriculture innovation in America of far-reaching importance, in that the invention enabled millers to take full advantage of the Spring wheats and their great strength. Because of their brittle skins which chipped and powdered when broken down—for washing them was unthought of—without a purifier a miller could not make from Spring wheat a flour of really first-class quality, or at all equal in colour to that made from Winter wheat. With a range of sieve and gravity purifiers, however, the millers could mill Spring wheats to great advantage as the offal specks in the fine middlings made by high grinding could be lifted out, and there grew up quickly a large host of willing customers for the big quantities of Spring wheat flour, which the Minneapolis and other mills of the Northwest turned out directly the farmers found there was a steady demand for the hard wheat they were growing, and thus if it had done nothing else its influence on the milling trade in this direction alone would have made the purifier a very remarkable machine.

The original purifying machines, if they should be called purifiers, were of the fanning type, but afterwards the gravity purifier came into use on the Continent, but the sieve type was followed in U.S.A., while both kinds were used in the U.K. Cabane's French machine was of the sieve type, but it was of a primitive kind, the sieve being composed of pierced parchment. It is interesting to note that the principle of the gravity purifier has been retained in many Continental mills, while in the United Kingdom it has not only been revived and used in more than one of the modern mills in pneumatic scalping systems, but for purification simply it has been almost discarded. Perhaps its best point was its simplicity. The semolina or middlings were fed over a feed gate in a broad thin line, through which a horizontal current of air was drawn. In the line of the air current was a number of baffle plates and deposit chambers and some adjustable valves. The force of the air playing against the feed naturally diverted all the particles to a greater or less extent. The heaviest and best middlings were, of course, deflected the least and fell almost straight down into the worm or collecting chamber. The lighter particles were deflected further and fell into the several deposit chambers, the heaviest being thrown down first and the lightest last. In this way the feed was separated into a number of portions ranged in the order of their specific gravity. The machine always did, and would do now good work on heavy stock—coarse or medium semolina for instance—but on fine middlings its limitations soon became very apparent, and it was impossible to make effective separations while there was a considerable invisible loss made. The gravity purifier was not used until very high grinding and fluted rolls were adopted. On the sieve purifier these fine stocks could be treated and the impurities eliminated in a very encouraging manner. In addition, the gravity purifier could separate only by differentiating between the specific gravity of the stocks it treated and not at all between their different sizes, while the sieve purifier, by employing both principles of separation at once, allows millers both to purify their stocks and at the same time in part to size them for the reductions.

The construction of the sieve purifier changed considerably during its early period of use. For a long time the aim of the builders was to improve the passage of the middlings along the sieve and to make the valves act correctly. The early machines were made to discharge the dusty air into special rooms, which were very objectionable from the insurance companies' point of view. Afterwards the aim of the builders of purifiers was to make a dustless machine, that is to say one that would blow its waste air into the purifier room quite free from dust. In this they were only partly successful, and to-day in place of the numerous big expansion and settling chambers, are found either machines working on the air belt system or else having a central fan working in connection with a dust collector, linked up by one main air trunk and various subsidiary ones to the several purifiers. By either method the invisible loss which is bound to occur to a greater or less extent, when the fans blow straight into the purifier room is avoided, much greater cleanliness and better health conditions are possible on the purifier floor, and when there is one central fan the machines can be made much smaller and there is thus a distinct saving both in the cost of construction and of space. Such are the advantages claimed for installing either air belt purifiers or a single exhaust in connection with the purifiers. It should be mentioned, however, that there are also a few debatable points. It is asserted by some that the constant use and re-use of the same air in an air belt machine must result in time in the air getting somewhat stale and a little contaminated. In reply, it is said that in such a case all that has to be done is to clean the machine regularly and that, provided the purifiers are cleaned out every shift, fresh air will then be admitted and then there can be no fear of trouble. Against the central exhaust installation there can be adduced the increased cost of installing a big fan and suction dust collector with the necessary trunk connections, and also the fact that the fan and suction filter consume slightly more power than do the purifiers which blow out into the room. Finally, it should be said that great care must be taken in arranging the air locking valves and devices in the main trunks or else every time the draught is altered in one compartment of a purifier the draught on all the other machines may be affected also. Such are some of the points the new methods of exhausting purifiers raise; the fact, however, that when new mills are put up the old so-called "dustless" purifiers are not usually put in, goes to show that the majority of the trade is of the opinion that the slight extra outlay involved by the new methods is quite justified.

Having said so much about the progress in the construction of a purifier—for the reader will be assumed to know the ordinary details of a modern machine—the question may be put as to why they are necessary at all, and why they are placed in the particular place in the flow sheet in which they happen to be found. And here it may at once be said that there are a few unorthodox millers who say that, provided the mixture is well enough cleaned and conditioned, the work the purifiers usually perform can be done equally well in other ways, and there may be a 'mill found here and there in which there are no purifiers. At the same time, under ordinary conditions with an ordinary system, and when a miller is not content with a medium quality straight run flour, but insists on having a good length of clear patents, it is not difficult to demonstrate the need for purifiers.

The sieve purifier belongs essentially to semolina milling. In the case of flour made specifically for baking by processes of chemical aeration, the production of semolina is of secondary importance—in fact, it is only of use as a means towards cleanliness, and has no value as a grader. In such a case the break system, as explained, may be subject to modifications, and purification may be satisfactorily attained in the improved or more extensive systems of scalping, dusting and dressing.

However, although proper conditioning has greatly reduced the work set the purifiers, and the number of impurities sent to them, the action of breaking down the berry is necessarily attended with considerable violence. As a result, even the best rollerman is bound to get some chips of bran of the same size as the semolina and middlings mixed up with them. The problem is, how can these impurities best be separated? They cannot be allowed to get into the flour sack. It has been suggested that by sending middlings and impurities both straight to a smooth roll, the impurities will be all flattened out, and thus will tail over the subsequent dresser, while the flour will be in no way affected. Undoubtedly something of this kind would occur and many of the offal particles would be flattened out, but without arguing the point as to how much the flour (patent) would be discoloured—and it is difficult to think the effect would not be noticeable—it must be remembered in such a case that the larger particles of offal would act as a cushion between the rolls and thus prevent them from reducing as many middlings into flour as they would if the latter were pure. The effect of this must be greatly to lessen the percentage of the high-grade flour that could be made on the early reductions. This in itself is a great point against the non-use of purifiers. When the colour question—which has not been discussed—is added, the case for the purifier—if it be in need of defence—becomes so much the stronger, for the purifier takes advantage of the precise difference that exists between the impurities, and the pure semolina and middlings, to separate them. By means of the air current each particle of feed that comes to a purifier can be weighed in a delicate balance, and that which is found wanting eliminated.

FLOUR DRESSING. .

CENTRIFUGALS AND PLANSIFTERS COMPARED.

The many operations relating to the preparation of the wheat berry for its subsequent transformation into flour, which have been explained in the previous chapters, culminate in that department devoted to the division of the products into grades for commercial sale purposes. All the work from that of the screensman, rollerman and purifierman upwards, right through the manufacturing process, leads up to the standard required, so that the resultant flour dressed out by the "silks" machines shall give satisfaction alike to mill proprietor, manager and, most important of all, the mill's customers. The work of the flour dressing department is second to none in its importance, and the standard of efficiency required to be possessed by the attendant on the " silks " floor is certainly not less than that which is sought from other operatives and machine attendants throughout the mill. Flour dressing is an essential adjunct to modern milling as practised on the roller process system and is one of the most important operations connected with the gradual reduction method of flour manufacture. The separation of the flour from the rolled product is the primary function of the "silks" machines and the "dressing" of the material is effected in various ways.

Reference has already been made to the early days of roller milling and in this connection we may be pardoned if we take cognisance of the early types of machines which did duty as flour dressers at that time. Just prior to the advent of the full automatic roller system, the machines used for dressing out the flour made on the millstones comprised a cylindrical reel (which was notable for its spaciousness as a dressing medium), also a selection of old style bolters and " wire dressers." Formerly the flour fresh from the " dressers " used to be run into " pastries," which latter consisted of apartments boarded up much after the style of the old-fashioned wheat bin used in the early days of wheat storage.

From the " pastries " the flour was invariably scooped up into sacks by the warehousemen upon receipt of an order and weighed out according to requirements. With the coming of the full roller process, however, the " pastry " system received its quietus, and in a large measure this was due to the fact that the flour made by the newer style of milling was cooler on leaving the " dressers " than that formerly made on the stone system. The idea of running the flour into bulk storage—as the " pastry " system can be legitimately termed—has not been lost sight of by some milling firms and, at least, one firm of milling engineers have adapted this system of storage for flour to meet present day requirements.

Adverting to the machines used for flour dressing purposes, these are practically confined in the modern mill to the two types of dressers at present in use, viz., the centrifugal and the plansifter. The former can be said to be the natural outcome of the old-fashioned reel, as the latter, by easy stages, may be said to have made the evolution of the centrifugal type easy by showing the improved class of work obtainable by the fitting of beaters, etc., in the type known as the inter-elevator reels. The inter-elevator reel held sway for a long time in the early nineties as a " gentle-treatment " scalper, and as such it was an improvement upon the common reel. Later the machine was used to a considerable extent as a flour dresser, but in this connection machines of this type generally gave place to the more efficient centrifugal as we know it at the present time. As its name denotes, the centrifugal works on the principle of dressing flour from the centre of the machine to its circumference. The centrifugal is covered round by a silk bolting cloth through which the flour particles are forced·by the action of the " dresser " The dressing action is accomplished by " finger-beaters," which are an unique feature of this type of flour dresser, and these beaters revolve round at a high rate of speed, doing their work efficiently when set at a proper angle with the axis of the machine shaft. The construction of the centrifugal, with which most young millers may be more or less familiar, centres round a main shaft which runs through the machine from end to end and rests on two bearings at either extremity, which in their turn are bolted to the framework of the machine. Upon the shaft is bolted a series of " spider " carriers to which the finger-beaters are attached, and the whole revolves at a high speed within an outer framework which revolves in the same direction as, but independent of, the main shaft, and at a much slower speed. The merits of the centrifugal as a flour dresser are well known, but a rival in the plansifter has been found, and this machine has many adherents who dispute the position occupied by the centrifugal and claim for the plansifter that its work as a dressing medium for flour justly entitles it to rank in the forefront of flour dressing machines along with the centrifugal.

The action of the plansifter is similar to that of the old hand sieve, and the principle embodied follows that old time adjunct to the trade. Mechanical difficulties for some time stood in the way of making the plansifter the success it was hoped for it as a flour dresser, but during recent years these difficulties have to a large extent been overcome. Those who favour plansifter flour dressing are perhaps in the minority in the trade, and the advocates of the plansifter have not verified the claim made some years ago that the days of the centrifugal were near a close. The chief difficulty in connection with plansifters was the amount of vibration imparted to the walls of a mill building, but the gyratory motion of the machine and improved methods of balancing have practically overcome this defect in construction. The plansifter is a combination of plane sieves banded, or clasped, together by tie rods so that the whole moves together as one piece of mechanism. The stock under treatment is fed on to an upper sieve and runs the gauntlet of six or more sieves—generally not exceeding twelve—during its travel through the machine. Each sieve makes a classification of stock and a great saving in space, power, and silk is thereby claimed for the plansifter as against the centrifugal.

One of the main objections to the plansifter is that the quantity of stock treated in a given time is limited, whereas the capacity of the centrifugal is a feature in its favour. The capacity of a plansifter is more subject to atmospheric influences than that of the centrifugal, and the condition of the wheat being ground must have special attention in a " plansifter mill "—more so than that necessary for a mill planned on the centrifugal system—to obtain success; in other words to maintain a good yield. A disadvantage in the use of plansifters for the purpose of flour dressing is that should a " break " occur in the silk it is necessary to stop the feed and the machine and take down the nest of sieves in order to repair the silk. Several attempts have been made to overcome this obvious hindrance to the successful adoption of plansifters, as flour dressers, and there are hopes that much headway may be made in this direction. The secret of successful flour dressing on plansifters is that a regular quantity of suitable ground product should be maintained upon the machine, also the exhausting arrangement for aerating the sieves should be kept in good working order, though the latter aid to successful flour dressing applies with equal force to the centrifugal and other units of machinery in the mill. The speed of the plansifters should remain constant as without proper attention in this regard no good work, or indeed any work, can be accomplished. The speed of the plansifter is approximately 180 revolutions per minute and at this speed good separation of stock can be attained. The centrifugal may be speeded to run about 200 to 250 revolutions and the silk clothing should be well stretched and laced up tight over the frame.

A difficulty with flour dressers working upon divided feeds of the same material is often encountered and forms one of the chief troubles of those whose duties it is to be in attendance upon the "silks" floor. The common practice where a feed has to be "split" so as to feed two or more machines is to insert a valve in the spout from the elevator leading to the dresser. This method, while simple enough, has its disadvantages as it cannot be said with any degree of certainty that the class of feed, though emanating from the same source, is identical going to each machine so fed. Especially is this true when the delivery spout from the elevator head to the flour dresser is built at an angle to meet erection difficulties. In most cases the feed will automatically divide itself in the course of its "fall," and one flour dresser will be found working upon rather heavier or more dense material than the other which will receive the lighter or more flocculent stock. Consequently the flour dresser in each case, though dressing out the same rolled product, will yield flour of different quality. This is a general source of annoyance to the silksman, and in an attempt to solve the problem of irregular product many silksmen try as an expedient the old-fashioned plan of sending rather more of the feed to the one machine that has the tendency to dress out bare. This practice is common in many mills, and the quality of the tailings coming from a flour dresser is the guide which is generally accepted as proof of the efficiency or otherwise of the machine.

Many operatives methodically incline to the practice of over-feeding one machine as against another in this regard and they probably act unconsciously in doing so and without understanding fully the technical cause of the variance of product from one machine compared with another treating similar stock. Where such dressing difficulties present themselves, due entirely to a wrong method of "feeding" the flour dresser, it is always advisable to arrange for a feed divider to be installed to overcome the irregular dressing. The "feed divider" is a small box-like apparatus fitted with a "Dawson" feed plate which is balanced and weighted in such a manner that a continuous stream of product to be dressed is evenly distributed between the two or more dressing mediums. The separation of flour from offal, which is the recognised duty of the flour dressing machine, is accomplished by an application of the principles of the laws of specific gravity in the first instance and subsequently by size.

In the centrifugal the action depends almost entirely upon the centrifugal force, and the particles of stock are caught by the beaters and immediately flung away from the circle described by them against the silk and if small enough they pass through its meshes. Centrifugals are usually clothed with coarser silks at the head of the machine, as it is here that the heavier floury particles are found making their way through the silk meshes according to the law of specific gravity which tends also to keep the lighter offal particles in suspense till the action of the beaters whips them forward to the next section. As the bulk of the flour will have been dressed out, and to keep the lighter particles from dressing through, a finer mesh of silk is thereby used on the second sheet and this maintains the colour feature by counterbalancing the tendency of fine offal to dress through owing to its coming into more or less direct contact with the silk by the absence of denser floury stock.

The same laws—specific gravity and size—govern the action of the plansifter and in the course of its travel through this machine the stock is graded into layers according to the specific gravity of the particles. The sieves of which the plansifter is itself constructed are set level and hence the name of the machine, *i.e.*, plane : sifter; sieves moving in the same plane. The plansifter is capable of making a great number of separations, and it takes up less room and requires less power to accomplish the same amount of work than centrifugals.

The duties of the " silksman " as the attendant is termed, who looks after these machines in the mill consists largely of maintaining regularity of product dressed out by these flour dressers. Watchfulness is essential on the part of the operative in charge here and the maintenance of belting in good running order and the oiling of the bearings on these machines require careful supervision. Samples require to be taken at regular intervals for due inspection and a record kept of " divides " so that the quality factor largely depends upon the efficiency of the silksman. Where percentages of divides are recorded and tabulated, the duty of keeping a book on these lines will form one of the duties of a good silksman in a modern mill.

A FEW NOTES ON CHEMISTRY AND PHYSICS
AS APPLIED TO MILLING.

The business of the miller is to produce for the public "the staff of life," ground into the form of flour, and to ensure that such flour shall be capable of producing, under the methods of panification used by his customers, a digestible, nutritious and wholesome loaf, pleasing both to the palate and the eye.

In order that he shall succeed in pleasing his *clientèle* and at the same time conduct his business with true intelligence, and at a profit, certain fundamental facts must be understood.

1. A thorough knowledge of the wheat berry and its various types.
2. How best to eliminate those portions of the grain not desired by his consumer.
3. How to make choice of wheats so that the blend will yield a flour which, when panified, shall produce a bread possessing sweetness of flavour and at the same time volume and proper "pile" in the crumb.

KNOWLEDGE OF THE WHEAT BERRY.

Wheat and its forbears has been in use as a food for man from the time of the earliest human records. It was regarded by the Egyptians as a gift to man by Isis, whilst the Greeks recognised Demeter as the donor. This goddess is better known under her Latin appellation "Ceres," and her name is commemorated in all Cereals : mythology also has it that Ceres taught mankind how to make bread.

Wheat is a monocotyledonous fruit, termed a Caryopsis. It belongs botanically to the sub-class Nudifloræ, and the sub-order Graminæ. It is the ripened ovary of the wheat blossom. The general character of the fruit is well known, but a sketch of a section of what millers call the "berry" will prove useful for reference.

Here we see the embryo plant, the germ, in juxta-position to the store of food provided for its sustenance during infancy, surrounded by a protective coating, the bran. When in the presence of a sufficiency of moisture, heat and air, the germ of life passes from the resting stage, to individual growth (such as is the case when wheat is sown in its most suitable nidus, viz., properly tilled, damp, warm soil) the infant plant pulsates with energy and soon commences to draw upon the store of food provided by nature, namely the proteins and carbohydrates contained in the endosperm. Like all forms of infant life, it needs its food prepared and brought to it. In the initial stages of development, the germ makes use of the small store of food present in its own body, and the plumule, and radicle commence to grow : when the stem and root have pierced the pericarp, the plant begins to draw upon the stored food of the endosperm, nature provides a channel of communication in the scutellum and absorptive epithelium, and solvent agencies, in the diastasic and proteolytic enzymes which are present. By means of these latter the starch and protein are rendered into soluble form. Both the altered starch and the altered protein are now able to pass through the provided chain of canal cells into the tissues of the growing plant, thus nourishing it during babyhood and until it is able to absorb the nourishment it requires from the soil.

The miller is not, however, directly interested in the growth of the wheat as a plant, but in rendering the berry into food for human kind.

A small proportion of the public, probably about four per cent., desire the whole wheat grain ground into meal. To provide for the needs of such consumers the millers' task is easy, he simply has to grind selected wheats to the necessary degree of fineness; but the vast majority of his clients demand that he shall provide for them a strong white flour, free from bran particles and the germ, which flour shall be

capable of standing the stress of yeast panification and capable also of standing reasonably long storage without losing
sweetness or stability. His object is, therefore, to make as
far as possible the following separation :

Endosperm.

Parenchymatous Cellulose.

Germ.

Bran, including the Aleurone cells.

The endosperm, freed from its parenchymatous tissue,
is essentially the "flour" of the miller, it contains the
whole of the Albuminoids, Fats, Sugars, Phosphates and
Carbohydrates natural to such.

The Parenchymatous tissue is removed in the processes
of reduction.

The germ has already been fully described, it is separated
in a condition of great purity; it is largely used in the preparation of specialised cereal foods.

The bran is eliminated as far as possible in the flaked
form, the remainder, with inseparable portions of the endosperm being included under the term of "sharps." The
chemical composition of the different products, determined
upon an average blend of wheat, of which the analysis is
first given, is as follows :—

	Wheat	Bran as milled	Sharps as milled	Germ as milled
Carbohydrates (including sugars) by difference ...	67·43	55·46	57·41	39·47
Albuminoids ...	15·07	15·97	15·09	27·73
Oil	1·86	4.37	4·98	12·04
Fibre	2·68	6·01	5·01	3·09
Ash	2·09	4·18	4·47	4·73
Moisture	11·87	14·01	13·14	12.94

In order that the complicated nature of the process by
which flour is converted into a loaf of bread may be appre-
ciated, there is recorded below a fuller analysis of an ordinary
flour followed by an enumeration of the substances which
are present when such flour is panified with yeast :

Starch by difference...	64·550
Cellulose ...	3·030
Albuminoids ...	13·880
Fat	1·460
Sugars ...	1·650
Dextrine	0·190
Gum, etc. ...	1·010
Carried forward...	85·770

Brought forward .		85·770
ASH consisting of—		
Potash ..	0·614	
Soda ..	0·044	
Lime ..	0·066	
Ferric oxide	traces	
Magnesia	0·236	
Phosphoric acid ...	0·910	
Sulphuric acid	0·007	
Silica	0·042	
Chlorine .. .	0·004	
		1·929
Lactic acid		0·151
Water		12·150
		100·000

The materials added by the action of yeast, and yeast itself :—

Glycerine.
Succinic Acid.
Butyric Acid.
Alcohols.
Carbonic Acid.
Acetic Acid.
Compounds of Nitrogen.
Chloride of Sodium (added salt).
"Vitamine."

It may be noted also that the quantity of various sugars in a given flour is greatly increased during the panification process, and also that there is an increase in the various phosphates and salts, owing to presence of such in yeast.

The demand by the majority of the public for the pure endosperm of wheat as the basis for the bread they desire, is undoubtedly the result of "natural selection" by them of the food which suits them best; the endosperm of wheat, when doughed, is capable of making a bread which possesses a minutely cellularised crumb (rendering it readily accessible to the gastric juices and hence digestible), and in addition has a sweet bland flavour, which blends well with the other portions of an ordinary mixed dietary, namely, meat, fish, etc. It must be noted, too, that white bread forms the natural complement to such mixed dietary, so that by a blend of such bread with meat, vegetables, etc., a well-balanced ration is obtained.

WHEAT AND THE FLOUR MILL.

When uncooked bran and germ are retained in the flour the active enzymes contained therein cause, during panification, excessive diastasic and proteolytic action, consequently the crumb of the resultant loaf is wanting in resiliency and accessibility to the digestive juices, and moreover there is imparted to the bread a strong flavour which interferes with the consumer's appreciation of the meat, etc., partaken of at the same time.

The fundamental reason, however, for the selection of wheat by man as the basis of his bread food, to the practical exclusion of all other cereals, is essentially due to the specific physical attributes possessed by its main nitrogenous constituents, namely, Glutenin and Gliadin

Wheat contains the following principal organic nitrogen compounds :—

Glutenin.
Gliadin.
Globulin.
Albumin.
Protein.

But it is to the first two that wheaten flour owes its characteristic power of forming, with water, and in the presence of the natural salts of wheat, a viscous medium in which the Carbonic Acid gas generated during the life process of yeast (or other means) can be imprisoned, vesiculation of the whole mass is thus obtained; when finally the dough is baked and the gas expanded, such vesicles become distended, and finely cellularised bread is produced.

The phenomena of the formation of " gluten " on the addition of water to flour is well known to all, the chemical actions involved in its production have been, and still are, the subject of much controversy. Two main theorems are put forward :—

1. That it is the result of the action of a body similar in character to myosin.
2. That (expressed in simple language) it is a simple hydration of two substances possessing a powerful

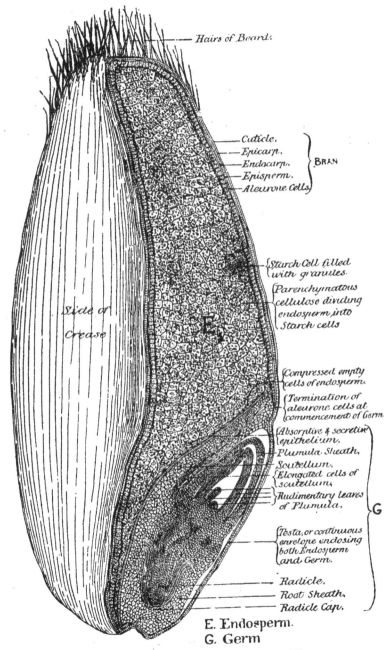

E. Endosperm.
G. Germ

LONGITUDINAL SECTION THROUGH A GRAIN OF WHEAT.
Magnified about 20 diameters.

Reproduced from a plate in Mr. W. Jago's book, "Technology of Bread Making," by permission of the author.

affinity for each other in the presence of water and the natural salts of the wheat.

The latter is the view that is considered most in accord with available evidence. The chemical composition of Gluten is well known and the determination of its elemental parts is easy to the chemist, moreover the purely elemental chemical composition of all wheat gluten, generally speaking, is practically alike.

The physical characteristics of gluten, however, vary greatly, and such differences are accentuated when the material is subjected to the stress of yeast panification.

Various theories are put forward to explain the known facts :—

1. That the main factor in determining the physical character and behaviour under panification is the relative proportion present of Glutenin and Gliadin.

2. That the presence or absence of salts of Phosphoric Acid is the principal factor.

3. That it is the presence or absence of excess of Amylolytic and proteolytic enzymes.

4. That it is an attribute of the relative electric condition of the proteins, the natural acids, and salts, and water.

Whatever be the final reason of "baking strength" there is no doubt but that it is a quality which is resident in the wheat Albuminoids, and there is little doubt but that it is the sum of various factors and not one simple attribute alone. An investigation of such a character as that of determining the final cause of baking strength, is one involving a prolonged series of elaborate tests, chemical and physical, and belongs to the domain of research chemistry, and is not a task such as can be properly undertaken in a miller's laboratory, neither is it likely to be a profitable investment, especially in view of the fact that a practical baking test can be made in a short space of time which is capable of giving at once positive information of immediate commercial value

As, however, apart from the mechanical side of milling, the most important study that a miller has to undertake is that of studying the blending together of different types of wheat so that (with due regard to cost) he can produce a flour which will satisfy the following legitimate demands of his customer, namely, that he shall produce a flour which shall be capable (when panified with water and yeast, under the particular method of panification used by his customer) of yielding a dough which on being handled by the baker, shall not give undue trouble in working and moulding up, and moreover that shall on being baked, yield the normal number of well-risen, well-piled loaves, sweet, and of agreeable flavour. To do this, constant care and thought is required.

In order to aid in the accomplishment of this object, what function can the chemist perform? As pointed out before, no royal or simple road exists by which the knowledge can be acquired. Carefully conducted taking tests are the true criteria, but the chemist, by continuous and thorough examination of the quantity and physical quality of the gluten collectable from the various wheats, and correlating the results obtained with the above referred to baking tests, can, in the course of time, render himself capable of forming opinions which should be of great assistance to his principals. Below, it is endeavoured to point out some of the ways in which desirable knowledge may be gained.

One outstanding and remarkable fact is that a given type of wheat, grown under the same conditions of environment (included under this term are climatic conditions, soil, time of sowing and reaping, etc.), generally speaking, produces a berry which is capable of yielding a flour which will always possess the same " baking character "; if any variation from the normal takes place in a given wheat, it is immediately shown by an important alteration in both the quality and character of the gluten.

If therefore the gluten from a given type of wheat from a given source be found to be normal, then the flour product from such wheat may be expected to, and will in fact fulfil, either by itself or in a blend, precisely the same function that experience has previously shown it able to perform.

If, on the contrary, abnormality in either quantity or

character is found to exist, then the miller is warned by his chemist, and it will behove him to test such wheat by the only certain method at present known, namely, by actual baking tests.

The following method of determining the quality and character of wheat and the gluten collectable therefrom will be found of service :—

WHEAT.

1. The sample should be thoroughly picked over, all foreign matters removed and weighed, and the quantity of smut, foreign seeds, etc., separately recorded.

2. The cleaned sample should be ground, firstly through a sharp set mill and secondly through a mill, the cones of which are only slightly cut. Twenty grams of such sample should be mixed with 100 ccs. of water, and the aroma carefully noted, the sample is then warmed in a hot water oven and again tested by the sense of smell—in both cases the product should be entirely free from any foreign odour.

3. The total ash determined.

4. The ground sample washed with ether in a Soxhlett tube, and the quantity of fatty matter recorded.

5. Two lots, each of 20 grams in weight, are taken and doughed with 12 ccs. of water (in a small Werner and Pfleiderer laboratory dough mixer by preference) and the viscosity of the dough carefully noted. One of the doughs is then allowed to stand exactly one hour, the dough is then washed in a porcelain dish with 250 ccs. of water, the mass being kneaded in the same water, until the whole of the gluten is agglomerated into a mass and all the starch and bran particles separated, the gluten mass is then thoroughly washed in fresh water, finally all the mechanically held water removed, and the resultant wet gluten weighed and its character carefully observed. A similar method is pursued with the second pat of dough which is, however, allowed to

stand for four hours, its character then noted and compared with first test.

6. The moisture content of the ground sample determined.

7. The bran substance present in the wheat is ascertained by the following method, viz., ten grams of the finely ground sample are mixed with 100 ccs. of water and heated in a water bath until complete gelatinisation is effected, the magma so produced is allowed to cool to say 80/90 degrees Fahr. To this is then added one gram of Taka diastase and the whole kept at a temperature of say 120/130 degrees Fahr. until complete saccharification is accomplished, the product is then boiled and finally filtered through a close linen filter, the residue collected, dried and weighed. From the weight of the residue so obtained the potential yield of flour obtainable from the wheat can be deduced.

8. The saccharine content of the wheat should also be found, both the mono and di saccharides.

9. Both the water soluble and the water insoluble phosphates should also be determined.

If a series of tests of the above character be carefully and regularly carried out and the data obtained, correlated with the results derived from practical working, experience and knowledge will be accumulated which will prove of great value.

At the present time, the simple tests given above, to which may be added the determination of the relative quantities of Glutenin and Gliadin, are those which are capable of yielding results, the bearing of which is at present understood by millers; while this represents the present position, there is nevertheless a vast field for work and discovery into the specific reasons which determine the baking value of a flour and exact and simply obtainable knowledge on this point would be greatly valued by all engaged in the wheat industry.

As an indication of the direction in which useful research

may be made, it is the opinion of the writer that the following are important factors in influencing the baking value of flours.

First, changes in the protein bodies present in flour due to concordant action between the flour itself and the yeast plant, with their accompanying enzymes, whereby they (the protein bodies) are rendered extensible and coagulable at a temperature approaching that at which egg albumen coagulates, thus simulating the characteristics of such egg albumen. In order that such action may take place, it is obvious that the protein bodies must be either autogenously capable of resolving themselves into a condition which allows of their passage through the cell wall of the yeast plant or the proteins must be themselves of such character that the yeast borne enzymes are capable of rendering them into like condition.

In either case the elaboration of the protein to an extensible and readily coagulable form allows of the fixation of the distended cells when the necessary temperature is reached during the process of baking.

Second : Assuming the presence in flour of a sufficiency of saccharine bodies to supply the needs of the yeast, it is known to be a desideratum that no undue amount of diastatic action shall take place, yet as the amount of sugars in well piled bread exceeds the quantity originally present, some diastase is apparently of value. What is the requisite quantity and exact kind of diastase desirable?

Third : Assuming the correctness of the hypothesis, that alcoholic fermentation involves the provision of hexose-phosphate, are there any special combinations of the natural wheat phosphates which favour the production of an ideal fermenting complex?

Do certain wheats contain bodies which are inimical to the formation of the desirable fermenting complex?

Are there present in desirable, and absent in non-desirable wheats protein bodies which are capable of entering into such, and does such combination induce strength?

Anyone entering into research work on this subject will

do wisely to obtain (if he has not already got them) the following books of reference :

Jago's " Technology of Bread Making."

The Monographs published by the Cambridge Schools of Biochemistry and of Agriculture, whose painstaking and enlightening work merits the gratitude of all engaged in the wheat industry.

T. B. Wood's Papers in the Agricultural Science Journals.

The " Vegetable Proteins," by Thomas B. Osborne.

The " General Character of the Proteins," by S. B. Schryver.

The various papers and data contributed by A. E. Humphries, Biffen and Wood.

A. D. Hall's Papers on Agricultural Science.

The above books will prove Guides, Philosophers and Friends to all earnest workers.

Whatever be the chemical or physical reason for Baking Strength," it appears to be a property which is dependent upon " race " and " environment." Race is important, but environment is undoubtedly the greatest factor. Healthy soil with a sufficiency of suitable food is an obvious necessity, and if those metabolic changes which result in the production of the desirable type of gluten are to take place the salts of the soil and the conditions of growth must be of the character to favour such formation. Assuming the correctness of Hofmeister's theory that the proteins are built up by the condensation of amino acids, it is clear that the conditions surrounding growth and development will greatly affect the particular types of amino acids formed, and consequently the exact type of protein produced, upon this point it is of great interest to note that Snyder has stated that Gliadin is not a definite compound. It is very probable therefore that under the name of Gliadin there have been included two or more similar bodies, the separation and recognition of which and the determination of their chemical and physical properties offers great promise to the investigator.

The effect of soil and environment is well exemplified by some work done by J. A. Le Clere and Sherman Leavitt, published for the International Congress of Applied Chemistry at Rome, a few extracts from such paper are given below :—

" The particular experiments whose results are herein recorded were started in 1905, with the collaboration of the Office of Grain Investigation of the Bureau of Plant Industry. They consist of growing continuously wheat (from the same original seed) in each of the three apices of a △, e.g., Kansas, Texas, and California, or South Dakota, Kansas and California. The crop from each apex is then sent to the other two stations and there grown alongside of the continuously-grown seed. We thus have three plots at each apex or station, all from the same original seed; one plot grown continuously at that point, and the other two plots coming from the other points of the triangle. We have styled them triangular experiments. Thus by this interchange of seeds we are enabled to determine the influence of climate and soil, and that of the seed on the composition of the crop."

" Two samples of wheat were used in our experiments : (a) Kubanka, a durum wheat and a spring variety grown in South Dakota, Kansas, and California; (b) a common wheat and a winter variety, Crimean, grown in Texas, Kansas, and California. The original Kubanka seed used for the South Dakota, Kansas and California triangle was grown in South Dakota in 1905, and sent to Kansas and California for the 1906 sowing, a sample likewise being grown in South Dakota in 1906. The crop thus obtained in each apex in 1906 formed the real starting point of the experiment. The South Dakota seed of 1906 was then sown in South Dakota in the Spring of 1907 and, further, a sample was sent to Kansas and one to California for the 1907 seeding. Likewise the 1906 Kansas crop was sent to South Dakota and California for the 1907 seeding, and seed was likewise sown in Kansas in 1907. The same was true with California seed. For the 1908 crops the seed used was that which had been obtained from the continuously-grown plot at each station. In exactly the same way a sample of Crimean was grown in Texas, Kansas and California, the original seed being grown in Kansas in 1905. Samples of each crop were collected and analysed for H2.0, ash P2.05, total N. Alcohol soluble N, salt soluble N, fat, fibre, pentosans, invert sugar, cane sugar, and the weight per bushel and the weight per 1,000 were taken, as well as the character and flinty or starchy condition of the grain.''

The tabulated results of such experiments are set forth on the following pages.

[TABLE I.]   SOUTH DAKOTA ORIGINAL SEED, 1905.

Protein—13·1%.   Wt per 1,000—37·2.   Weight per bushel—62·8.   Flinty—70·0.

	KANSAS 1906 From South Dakota 1905 seed	CALIFORNIA 1906 From South Dakota 1905 seed	SOUTH DAKOTA 1906 From South Dakota 1905 seed
Protein	19·8	9·7	14·2
Weight per 1,000	30·4	41·7	357
„ per bushel	56·8	60·0	613
Flinty	100·0	13·0	70·0

	KANSAS 1907			CALIFORNIA 1907			SOUTH DAKOTA 1907		
	From Kansas 1906 seed	From California 1906 seed	From South Dakota 1906 seed	From Kansas 1906 seed	From California 1906 seed	From South Dakota 1906 seed	From Kansas 1906 seed	From California 1906 seed	From South Dakota 1906 seed
Protein	Lost	Lost	Lost	9·7	10·0	9·1	14·2	13·9	12·9
Weight per 1,000	—	—	—	43·8	41·4	39·1	38·7	37·9	39·4
„ per bushel	—	—	—	61·8	62·0	61·5	62·2	63·0	63·7
Flinty	—	—	—	22·0	29·0	88·0	99·0	98·0	88·0

	KANSAS 1908			CALIFORNIA 1908			SOUTH DAKOTA 1908		
	From Kansas 1907 seed	From California 1907 seed	From South Dakota 1907 seed	From Kansas 1907 seed	From California 1907 seed	From South Dakota 1907 seed	From Kansas 1907 seed	From California 1907 seed	From South Dakota 1907 seed
Protein	13·3	13·1	13·5	14·6	13·5	14·0	15·5	15·0	14·8
Weight per 1,000	30·8	30·5	31·8	37·7	44·8	36·3	25·8	24·9	29·8
„ bushel	57·8	55·2	53·8	30·0	61·2	59·4	59·0	57·8	60·2
Flinty	100·0	96·0	98·0	100·0	100·0	100·0	100·0	100·0	100·0

[TABLE II.]

KANSAS ORIGINAL SEED.

Protein—16·2%.   Weight per 000—21·1.   Weight per bushel—56·5.   Flinty— 8·9.

	KANSAS 1906 From Kansas 1905 seed	OHIA 1906 From Kansas 1905 seed	TEXAS 1906 From Kansas 1905 seed
Protein	19·2	10·4	12·1
Weight per 1,000	22·7	34·0	30·6
„ bushel	58·8	59·4	58·9
Flinty	000·0	36·0	100·0

	KANSAS 1907			CALIFORNIA 1907			TEXAS 1907		
	From Kansas 1906 seed	From California 1906 seed	From Texas 1906 seed	From Kansas 1906 seed	From California 1906 seed	From Texas 1906 seed	From Kansas 1906 seed	From California 1906 seed	From Texas 1906 seed
Protein	22·2	22·8	22·2	11·0	11·3	11·4	17·0	18·2	18·2
Weight per 1,000	20·5	21·3	20·5	33·8	33·3	33·0	23·6	22·7	23·6
„ bushel	51·3	51·3	50·7	61·3	61·8	62·3	58·6	57·3	58·6
Flinty	100·0	100·0	100·0	50·0	60·0	50·0	98·0	100·0	95·0

	KANSAS 1908			CALIFORNIA 1908			TEXAS 1908		
	From Kansas 1907 seed	From California 1907 seed	From Texas 1907 seed	From Kansas 1907 seed	From California 1907 seed	From Texas 1907 seed	From Kansas 1907 seed	From California 1907 seed	From Texas 1907 seed
Protein	14·5	14·9	Lost	11·6	12·0	12·6	Lost	Lost	Lost
Weight per 000	28·4	28·8	—	33·0	32·8	33·6	—	—	—
„ bushel	58·1	58·2	—	61·7	61·4	60·2	—	—	—
Flity	99·0	99·0	—	95·0	95·0	95·0	—	—	—

WHEAT AND THE FLOUR MILL.

The following *resumé* of tests is given, in which the results are more closely correlated, with additional data as to the sugar content, from the original table the figures for weight per bushel and the proportion of flinty wheat is deleted.

[TABLE III.]

	Protein	Sugars	Weight per 1,000
KUBANKA.			
South Dakota 1906— California 1907 ...	9·1	4·4	39·1
California 1906—California 1907	10·0	4·9	41·4
South Dakota 1907—California 1908 ...	14·0	4·4	36·4
California 1907—California 1908	13·5	4·4	44·3
California 1906—South Dakota 1907 ...	13·9	3·8	37·9
South Dakota 1906—South Dakota 1907...	12·9	3·7	39·4
California 1907—South Dakota 1908 ...	15·0	3·6	24·9
South Dakota 1907—South Dakota 1908..	14·8	3·9	29·8
CRIMEAN.			
Kansas 1906—California 1907	11·0	4·1	33·3
California 1906—California 1907	11·3	3·9	33·3
Kansas 1907—California 1908	11·6	3·5	33·0
California 1907—California 1908	12·0	3·5	32·8
California 1906—Kansas 1907	22·8	2·9	21·3
Kansas 1906 - Kansas 1907	22·2	3·0	20·5
California 1907—Kansas 1908	14·9	2·9	28·8
Kansas 1907—Kansas 1908	14·5	3·0	28·4

weight per bushel and the proportion of flinty wheat are the paper in its entirety should be consulted, and the convincing evidence contained therein carefully mastered.

The effect of manuring the soil for wheat growing is an interesting and important study; all possible means should be taken to provide those substances which assist proper nitrogenous development.

Nature should be aided in producing a wheat (if possible in our country) which is in itself capable of satisfying the demands of the miller and his customers.

146

While nature fails to supply the ideal wheat in sufficient quantity, the miller must, by blending, try to rectify nature's deficiencies. How far the miller is justified in endeavouring to supply such deficiencies by subjecting wheat or flour to conditions which induce changes by the encouragement of enzymic or other nitrogenous action, by processes of conditioning, by acceleration of changes in the colouring bodies, or by directly counteracting shortages in the bodies necessary to the fermenting complex, this has been the subject of much controversy, but it seems to the writer that if the golden rule of life be applied and it be found that any contemplated treatment is in the best and full sense of the expression, not to the prejudice of the consumer, then it surely must be right that millers should be allowed to advantage themselves of the advancement of scientific knowledge, such advantage being accorded to the producers of foodstuffs generally.

The task of attempting to set forth within a small compass the main points relative to chemistry as applied to milling is an extremely difficult one, the subject in its various aspects being so vast. It is hoped, however, that the few data contained in the foregoing article will prove of interest, and have the effect of stimulating to a closer study by milling students, of the chemical and physical side of their art.

THE BLEACHING OF FLOUR.

A CHEMIST'S VIEW.

The following is an endeavour to describe the purely chemical aspect of the bleaching of flour. First of all, one may summarise the conditions from which follow the dark colour of flour of certain kinds.

1. The more or less intense yellow of the endosperm of some varieties of wheat.
2. The grinding up and inclusion in the flour of portions of the dark coloured outer coverings of the wheat grain.
3. The grinding of dirty wheat, *i.e.*, wheat soiled with outside dirt, and incorporating same in the flour.

Taking the last two of these first, one may at once point out that the remedy for No. 2 is the use of adequate methods of separation during the milling process; and in fact well made flour is practically free from branny particles, except in the case of the very lowest grades. The remedy for dirty wheat is still more self-evident, and simply consists of thorough cleaning. Modern wheat cleaning processes are so efficient that there is little excuse for the production of dirty and dark coloured flours through the milling of dirty wheats. These causes of dark coloured flour may therefore be summarily dismissed.

There only remains the first-mentioned cause of colour, that of the endosperm or floury matter of the wheat itself. It is well known that wheats vary very considerably in this respect. To take an actual example, the flour of Californian wheat is practically white, while that of Walla-Walla wheat is a full dark yellow. In other respects the two flours may be regarded as identical in character, and yet, because of the colour only, the former has a considerably higher value on the market than has the latter.

148

At this stage one may very well inquire as to what such colouring matter is really due. Monier-Williams in the Laboratory of the Local Government Board subjected this matter to considerable investigation and arrived at the conclusion that the colouring matter of flour seems to be identical with carotin, the yellow colouring matter of carrots. Carotin is a highly unsaturated hydrocarbon of a somewhat unstable character, and by the action of oxygen is transformed into comparatively colourless bodies. As a result of this, flour distinctly improves in colour as the result of age, and the problem arises whether a similar improvement could be effected by other means.

The nature of the problem which presented itself to investigators was whether there was any means of discharging this colour of the full yellow flour without in any way injuring the flour in other particulars. This question was in the first place urged upon the writer by one of the most respected men in the Liverpool flour trade. To mention his name is sufficient proof of this; the gentleman referred to was the late Mr. Paul, of Messrs. Ross T. Smyth & Co. A consequence of this conversation was an investigation by the writer of the action of a number of decolourising agents on flour. These narrowed themselves down to a group of oxidising agents, and finally ozone was selected as the most promising substance.

Ozone has a very decided decolourising action on flour, but unfortunately at the same time introduces an unpleasant flavour or taint by which it is rendered unfit for use. Subsequently, Frichot, a French inventor, in 1898 recommended and patented the use of electrically developed ozone for the same purpose, but again the unpleasant flavour imparted rendered the process commercially unsuccessful.

The next step in flour bleaching consisted in the discovery of nitrogen peroxide as a suitable decolourising agent. Like ozone, this is an oxidising substance but, unlike it, does not impart any objectionable flavour to the flour. The credit for this invention lies with Andrews, of Belfast, and accordingly in January, 1901, Letters Patent were granted to John and Sydney Andrews for what in effect was the improvement in flour due to treatment with nitrogen peroxide gas. The method employed consisted in the production of the gas by the action of ferrous sulphate on nitric acid; after which the flour was passed, by means of a conveyor, through a current of air containing the bleaching gas in small quantity. Almost instantaneously the yellow colour of the flour was discharged, and simultaneously the ruddy tint of the gas disappeared.

A further advance was made in 1903 when Alsop patented an improved process in which the nitrogen peroxide was produced by the passage of a flaming discharge of electricity through air. In this way the purely chemical process of preparing the peroxide by the use in a mill of such a very active chemical re-agent as nitric acid was avoided.

By this time the bleaching of flour had become a recognised commercial process.

The nature of the chemical change was regarded as one in which the colouring matter, carotin, was oxidised to a colourless substance by the action of nascent oxygen yielded by the peroxide. The treated flour was found to contain nitrites, and so the probable initial chemical change, in the presence of moisture, was regarded as the following :—

$$2NO_2 + H_2O = 2HNO_2 + O$$

| Nitrogen peroxide. | Water. | Nitrous acid. | Nascent oxygen. |

Or, putting it another way, nitrogen peroxide, N_2O_4 lost an atom of oxygen to the colouring matter and became N_2O_3, nitrous anhydride, which in turn combined with water and formed nitrous acid, HNO_2. Subsequently, the nitrous acid united with some one or other of the bases present in flour, and so formed a nitrite (salt). Snyder inclines to the belief that the combining base is ammonium, in which case ammonium nitrite, NH_4NO_2, would be formed.

Another view of the action was that the nitrogen peroxide might be absorbed by some part of the flour as a whole, and so an actual nitration of colouring matter and possibly proteins of flour could take place. As to what changes might be effected by over-dosing flour with the peroxide lies rather outside the present subject, but with normal bleaching the action seems confined to one of oxidation and formation of nitrites. In bleaching action as conducted by millers, it is not the practice to completely discharge the yellow colour of the flour : in other words, the colouring matter is usually in slight excess and therefore the action is regarded as one of oxidation.

An alternative suggestion is that the nitrogen peroxide is reduced by the colouring matter of the flour to nitrogen dioxide, thus—

$$NO \quad = \quad NO \quad + \quad O$$

Nitrogen	Nitrogen	Nascent
peroxide.	dioxide	oxygen.

In accordance with its well-known properties the dioxide would combine with free oxygen present, again to become nitrogen peroxide, and thus the peroxide might act indefinitely as a carrier of repeated quantities of oxygen to the flour. Nitrogen peroxide does in fact act in this way as a carrier of oxygen in other well-known chemical processes. The subsequent finding of nitrites in the flour rather points, however, to the first being the usual reaction.

The introduction of bleaching processes led to the expression of widely different opinions by chemists who interest themselves in articles of food. There is one school of chemical thought which is of the persuasion that the long-recognised and legitimate modes of manufacture should be adhered to, and the introduction of chemical meddling with food materials resisted, and such treatment should not be left to the discretion of the manufacturers of food. Another school of chemists takes the view that it is the manufacturer's business to make good food, and as long as he sells it for what it is he is at perfect liberty to remove any objectionable constituents which impair its qualities. As between the two it is only fair to remember that the manufacture of foods, in common with that of most other commodities, has been slowly progressive in its developments, as the result of the application of improvements devised by the manufacturers themselves. It would therefore seem scarcely logical to step in at any moment and say flour shall consist of a body made by the methods so far devised and gradually adopted by millers; but they (the millers) shall not be permitted to employ any further improvements they may invent or discover.

The representatives of the first-named school of chemists were up in arms against this introduction of bleaching, and made all sorts of allegations against such treatment of which in many cases the wish was probably father to the thought.

Thus one American observer states officially that bleaching has the following ill effects :—(1) An injurious substance in the form of nitrites is left in the flour; (2) The oil from well-bleached flour on storage has a rancid odour and character, whereas the oil from a similar flour unbleached was wholesome and not rancid; (3) Bleaching has a marked injurious effect upon the gluten; (4) An unbleached flour which absorbed 69.5, per cent. of water when bleached absorbed only 64 per cent. The same authority states that there is produced in flour as the result of artificial bleaching, toxic bodies; further, that there are indications of the possibility of the formation of diazo compounds when flour has been subjected to bleaching, especially when bleaching has been carried to a considerable extent. On making alcoholic extracts from unbleached flour and feeding same to rabbits they were not affected, but on making alcoholic extracts in the same way from commercially bleached flour and feeding rabbits thereon, their death was thereby caused in a few hours. Other writers have pointed out that the nitrites in bleached flour may be a source of harm to some individuals instancing that half a grain may in such cases be injurious, while what may be the effect of smaller doses taken day by day throughout many months or years it is impossible to say. In a well-known Local Government Board Report it is, moreover, definitely laid down "that in the case of flour which is bleached to the small extent which is at present ordinarily practised, it would in present knowledge be unwise to conclude that the process is attended by absolute freedom from risk.'' Subsequently, however, the chemical officials of this Department seem to have thought this particular attitude was a little overdone, as Monier-Williams (one of the contributors to the Report referred to) at a meeting of the Society of Public Analysts made the following remark : '' He thought that in proceedings relating to bleached flour, the question of the deleterious action of nitrites themselves had been given rather too much prominence, because it was open to the defence to say that the actual quantity of nitrite present was too minute to have any physiological effect.''

More robust was the reply of Wesener and Teller to these various allegations. Dealing with the nitrite bogey, they point out that the highest quantity in bread from bleached flour is 0.0000025 per cent., or 0.025 parts per million, while rain water contains 0.000171 per cent., or 70 times as much as bleached flour bread. Again, ham bought in the open market contains about 500 times as much. The maximum safe dose of nitrite is three grains (0.19 grams), which is equivalent to 0.1 gram of nitrogen trioxide. In order to consume this quantity of nitrogen trioxide by eating the bread from bleached flour, 10,000 one pound loaves would have to be eaten. At the average rate of bread consumption, an individual who commenced the day he was born would be 55 years old before he would thus have taken a single medicinal dose of nitrogen trioxide. Further, the writers do not find the oil or the gluten of flour to be injured by bleaching, nor is there even the slightest change in any of the other proximate principles of flour. It may also be pointed out that dark flours have a higher food value in the estimation of some scientists than have whiter flours. By bleaching such flours they are made more acceptable to the public. Consequently, flour bleaching does not permit the substitution of an inferior article for a superior one, but on the contrary makes more suitable for use articles which otherwise are in a measure objectionable.

A very searching examination of the effect of bleaching

on flour was made by Snyder and the results published as a Bulletin by the University of Minnesota. His principal results may be thus summarised :—The fat of flour is unaltered by bleaching; that is its iodine absorption number, nitrogen content, and heat of combustion are practically the same whether the flour is bleached or unbleached. The gluten and gliadin are unaffected by the bleaching process. Next, Snyder puts his finger on the crucial point of all tests on bleached flour, viz., what results are found in the *bread*? As stated by him, flour is never eaten in the raw state, but is always prepared for food by being subjected to the action of heat. During this heating the nitrite re-acting material is removed and the bread and other articles of food give no re-action for nitrites. Since the material used in the bleaching of flour is expelled in the preparation of the food, there remains no question for physiological consideration. Snyder insists that the bleaching of flour is a process perfectly analogous to the bleaching of sugar in course of manufacture. Snyder concludes by asserting that in bread-making tests of commercially bleached flour no difference whatever was observed between the breads produced from the bleached and the unbleached flours milled from the same wheats, except that the bleached flours produced a whiter bread and also showed a tendency to produce larged sized loaves. Bleaching of the flour did not impart any odour or taste to the bread or leave in it any residue.

Obviously the addition of, say, 0.00002 per cent. of nitrites to a flour cannot appreciably affect its general composition, so that no question arises as to nutritive value. As to digestibility, Snyder made some minute tests as to the differences, if any, between bleached and unbleached flours. He found no difference whatever in digestibility between the two.

The question of the possible presence of poisonous diazo compounds in flour as a consequence of bleaching has been made the subject of careful experiment by Wesener and Teller; the results have in every case been absolutely negative, and no trace of such poisonous bodies could be discovered.

The statement that bleached flour yielded an extract which was fatally poisonous to rabbits was deliberately advanced in a patent action tried before Mr. Justice Warrington in 1909. This led to the other side calling in two medical experts to repeat the experiments. In the course of his judgment Mr. Justice Warrington said :—" Dr. Wilcox and Dr. Luff, who are two of the most eminent men in their branch of the medical profession, have made experiments on rabbits with concentrated extracts of flour bleached under the plaintiff's process . and they have kept those rabbits under observation for many days after the administration, and have observed no effect on the rabbits beyond a temporary intoxication caused by the fact that the extract was alcoholic." In this case every scrap of evidence for and against the effect of bleaching was adduced, and the final decision of the learned Judge becomes therefore of all the more value.* It was expressed in the following terms :—" It seems to me, therefore, that, whether you regard it from the point of view of digestion, whether you regard it from the point of view of nutrition, or whether you regard it from the point of view of positive harm, I must come to the conclusion that the plaintiffs have established the truth of the statement . . that no deleterious action on the flour is caused by the above-mentioned [bleaching] treatment."

Having disposed of the general question of the result of bleaching on the welfare of the community, there remains the lesser problem of how the interests and difficulties of bakers are thereby affected. The following is a much condensed summary of objections raised to bleaching by some of its opponents :—It is possible to conceal defects in flour made from unsound grain, and to make the flour from dark coloured wheats resemble that from high class wheats. It is further said that bakers rely largely upon the appearance of the flour in judging its quality; they are thereby misled in their judgment. Again, the baking qualities of the flour are prejudicially affected from the first, and become so modified that the baker is no longer able to rely on those appearances and characteristics of fermentation which enable him to regulate that operation.

So far as dark colour and unsoundness go together, the present writer has never had an instance brought before him, professionally or otherwise, of unsoundness being masked by bleaching. If dark flour is made white, that is not concealing, but removing an inferiority; in just the same way as the conversion of dark brown into white sugar is a definite improvement and not the concealment of a defect. If bakers rely on the colour of their flour as an indirect guide to its other qualities, this is rather a pity, since absolutely natural flours of the same colour may differ remarkably in other qualities, and flours of naturally very different colours may be practically identical in every other property. In any case every careful baker supplements his judgment by appearance by a baking test on the flour, and this reveals the qualities and defects of any sample. When bleaching was first adopted there is no doubt it introduced a new factor, which came somewhat as a surprise on the baker's judgment, but no greater, for example, than that caused by the substitution of the long length patents of the roller system for the much shorter patents of millstone milling. In all such cases the competent baker's judgment rapidly adapts itself to the new conditions, and at the immediate pre-war moment, when colour was really a factor in flour values, the baker found no difficulty though bleaching had been so largely adopted.

With regard to the effect on baking qualities and fermentation of flour, the present writer made in 1903 what was, he believes, the first set of systematic baking and chemical tests which were ever published on bleached flour. Altogether seventeen samples were thoroughly analysed and baked. Bleaching seems to have had very little effect on general behaviour during fermentation. What effect there was was in the direction of their working better and holding up better. The writer summarised his conclusions in the following :—" It is not safe to generalise on so few

THE BLEACHING OF FLOUR.

experiments, but so far as they have gone they point to a possible softening and mellowing of very hard flours, without a corresponding softening of flours which are already sufficiently soft   . In making baking tests, the water absorbing power of most flours seems to be slightly increased. With the very soft flours there is no very great difference observable in their behaviour during fermentation, which rather bears out the view that their gluten is not further softened by the process. But in the case of the hard flours, they are found to work more freely and to make a larger and bolder, and at the same time better shaped loaf.''

The writer has never found any commercial baker who regards the advent of bleached flour as having materially affected his judgment in forming an opinion on the progress of fermentation and baking operations generally. The fact is, the variations caused in the same flour by the act of bleaching are much less than those necessarily caused by alterations in the wheat mixture or modifications in the milling processes.

The writer most cordially agrees with the conclusion expressed by Dr. Hamill on p.p. 18/19 of the Local Government Report on Flour Bleaching :--'' While plants for bleaching are possessed by a limited number of millers, the latter may undoubtedly be at an advantage over many millers not so circumstanced, so long as bakers and the public continue to attach importance to the whiteness of flour regardless of the manner in which the whiteness is produced. Should the practice become universal, however, and bleaching become an additional process which all millers have to employ, this advantage would disappear.''

The whole history of milling developments and progress has been one in which the milling trade has expended many hundreds of thousands of pounds on the adoption of improvements. After some very slight reward to the pioneers, the benefits are evenly divided among millers. To paraphrase the words of Dr. Hamill but very slightly :— The benefits of bleaching, like those of other milling improvements, are very shortly reaped by the general public without either fee or reward.

THE BLEACHING OF FLOUR.

A BAKER'S VIEW.

The public like white bread because its appearance induces the impression of purity, or at least of cleanness : each baker is anxious to please as large a section of the public as he can, and endeavours to make his bread white. Roller milled flour easily supplanted stone milled, because of its " good " colour, and for the same reason, as milling processes improved, top grades were more in favour than " straights." When in the stress of competition millers adopted bleaching processes, the baker hesitated as to whether he should acclaim the improvement or not. The public desire for whiteness, and the bakers' anxiety to meet it, is at the best only a comparative feeling : people like bread whiter than the dark stuff of the olden time, or say, of war time, but after a certain intensity of whiteness is reached greater whiteness has no value to the consumer, and therefore none to the baker. The latter is well aware that a high class flour, made from suitable wheat, needs no bleaching of its top grades, and he doubts if the public really prefer chalky whiteness to that which has in it a dash of a creamy tint. In any case, it is the common experience in the baking trade that, given good flavour, and a bright appearance in crumb and crust, then excessive whiteness of bread brings no special satisfaction to customers.

From the beginning of the bleaching period the baker has been suspicious of the miller's operations in this matter, but for commercial rather than for technical reasons. As an expert he is quite well aware that it is not colour only that constitutes the value for bread-making purposes of the highest grade flours; he finds in them the virtues that give to the crumb of his loaf a nice sheen and a velvety softness, and to the crust a golden brightness, which qualities are all difficult to produce with lower grade flours. But the method of determining grade by cursory examination, even when flour is bought on sample, is almost solely by colour, while the subtle indications in the baked bread to which reference has just been made are not readily detected, or, at any rate, slight faults if discovered are as likely and as justly to be ascribed to the vagaries of the baker's own processes as to the quality of the flour. If there is reference even to orthodox chemical tests, their possible unreliability has been impressed on the baker by reports of cases in the courts, in which scientists of repute gave testimony so opposed that judges have been unable to determine in what appeared quite simple cases whether the flour under consideration had been artificially bleached or not. When buying flour that has possibly been bleached, the baker's consciousness of his helplessness to protect himself fans his suspicions : he fears that he may be buying a second grade flour, or even one lower in the scale, at the price of a top grade, and when he makes a contract he wonders whether the new deliveries are only as white as the original but not quite of the same grade.

It is a generally accepted rule that low grade flours cannot be bleached to improve them, but this knowledge has not prevented some millers from making the attempt. Some years ago when the " Apostoloff Bread Company " started operations in London, an electrical bleaching plant was installed, possibly for spectacular purposes, and a straight grade flour, crudely made, was bleached. The bread was of the worst possible colour for bread; it was a very dull gray in both crust and crumb. Bleached low grade flour has been sold to bakers in considerable quantity since that time, but not to the satisfaction of either baker or miller.

In a technical sense the influence of bleaching of flour by the ordinary method with nitrous oxide gases, whether these are prepared from the air by electrical methods or by ordinary chemical means, is not very pronounced, if the bleaching has not been overdone. As the flour is, so the bread is appreciably whitened in crumb, and the crust is made just a little lighter in colour than they would be if the same flour unbleached had been used. In addition to these colour changes, it has been proved by many experiments of a purely practical kind, that bleaching, for some reason not properly determined, slightly accelerates the ripening process in dough, and that, in consequence, a dough made with bleached flour will be ready for scaling sooner by about ten per cent. of the total time than one made from the same flour unbleached, the quantity of water, salt and yeast, and the temperature being alike in both cases. As the nitrous gases have no accelerating effect on yeast action, this observed result must be due to the slight changes produced on the gluten of the flour by these gases, an effect that evidently reduces its resistance to the softening action of the yeast and other enzymic agents present in the dough. Support is provided for this idea by the fact that in cases in which flour is overbleached the results in dough and in bread are identical with those produced by overfermentation in the ordinary process with unbleached flour. If two doughs are in all respects alike, but one is made from bleached and the other from the same flour unbleached and these doughs are allowed time in trough so that only the one with bleached flour is ready for scaling; and if both doughs are then scaled, the loaves of the unbleached dough are likely to be smaller than the other, and to show the usual signs of unripeness in the bread; on the other hand, if both doughs wait until that with the unbleached flour is ready, the loaves from the bleached flour will be slightly overripe and such state will be indicated by a tendency to crumbliness.

It is a miller's rather than a baker's problem how much gas should be incorporated with the flour to produce effective and safe bleaching, and how much constitutes the dose for overbleaching, but the results of certain baking tests with flour containing known quantities of gas should not be without interest to both parties. The gas used for bleaching was produced by the action of strong sulphuric acid on potassium nitrite. Into four lots of flour there was respectively passed quantities of nitrogen peroxide gas

(NO_2) equivalent to 1.2, 2.4, 4.4 and 9.14 parts in 10,000 of flour. The bleaching was quite pronounced in the case of No. 1 and showed a gradual change from chalky white to decided gray in the case of the others. The dispute as to whether the change of colour is due solely to the decolourising of the oil of the flour, or to a change in the colour of the gluten toward grayness, is not settled by carefully washing the wet gluten from the flour, because the oil constitutes a part of this crude gluten. But, in any case, the crude gluten as obtained from these flours, with all precautions against darkening while washing, showed that the gradations of change toward gray are distinctive and regular; No. 4, after lying a little, appearing quite black. The explanation of a whitening effect accruing from a darkening of one of the colouring constituents of the flour is that the change is in fact an optical effect similar to that following the addition of a small quantity of blue to icing sugar, or to starch in laundry work.

The doughs made from the four flours, with a batch made from unbleached for comparison, exhibited the signs of quicker ripening in proportion to the amount of gas used : the loaves with the higher quantity were dull on crust and gray in crumb, and the latter was very friable. Reference was made above to the effects following excessive bleaching. If the process is allowed to proceed considerably past the highest just noticed, the crude gluten of the flour, as washed out in the usual way with cold water, is reduced in quantity below the normal, and bread made from such flour is distinctly gray in colour of crumb, flat, and with dark cracks on the outside, similar to the signs appearing when loaves are made from dough that has been very much overripened. It is interesting to note, that in dough, yeast and the other active agencies at work produce bleaching action about the same in effect as the gas used by millers to whiten flour. At the stage bakers know as " ripe " the dough is considerably whiter than when first made; at the stages of over and excessive ripeness the approach to dull white first and then to gray is easily noticeable. If gluten is washed from

from definite weights of the dough at the several stages, the proportion becomes perceptibly reduced, and the colour is darkened. These changes appear to vary directly, as the fermentation proceeds from normal to great excess.

The claim of those who favour bleaching of flour, that it thereby is sterilised, and that it gives an increased yield of bread does not appeal strongly to the baker. Experiment have shown that bread made from bleached flour is not immune from the one disease that has special terrors for the baker, viz., "rope," and as for the action of other possible germs in flour, there is not any evidence that in normal breadmaking they are hurtful unless the fermentation processes are allowed to proceed too far. As for increased yield, ostensibly due to the drying action of the bleaching gas, the change must necessarily be so minute as to be negligible.

There are other flour bleaching or whitening processes in which other gases than nitrogen peroxide are used, but for reasons concerned with the residue products in the flour they are not now used commercially. In the case of some bread improvers, notably those containing persulphates, a certain quantity of oxygen is set free while the dough is fermenting and the bread baking, and this oxygen has a slight bleaching effect. At the same time it is claimed that the persulphates otherwise toughen the gluten of the flour, and ensure a loaf of larger volume. Experiments with persulphates show that while they do very slightly intensify whiteness, they also, like bleaching by gas, tend to ripen the dough at a rate above the normal.

Other compounds of a more or less astringent nature in certain circumstances do whiten bread, but without bleaching. Alum for instance, and certain other sulphates like Epsom and Glauber's salts. Some phosphates have a like effect, particularly that of ammonia. As these have some effect on the yeast, as well as on the materials of the dough, their action is complicated, but the whitening effect is principally physical, due in fact to improvement in the texture and volume of the loaf. Those agents that accelerate fermentation will produce an apparent whitening effect, as compared with a loaf of rougher texture or smaller volume, while accelerated yeast action, as already noticed, does whiten the dough. The character for whitening which alum secured was obtained at a time when doughs were "runny" and in consequence the bread was dark. Alumned bread with more stability appeared white. Slightly bleached flours do not worry the baker : overbleaching through ignorance or accident would spoil his bread.

EVERY CLASS AND
DESCRIPTION OF

CHEMICALS
used by MILLERS

═══════════════ *are made by* ═══════════════

VICTORS, LTD.,
Sutton Oak Works, ST. HELENS.

Head Office - - - - - 16, Deansgate, Manchester.

SPECIALITY ·

PURE ACIDS FOR SELF RAISING
FLOUR.

IMPROVERS FOR WEAK FLOURS.

"Eureka" Grain Cleaning Machines.

"Eureka" Perfected Milling Separator, with Centrifugal Disc Dust-proof Eccentric.

New Perfected Receiving Separators, with Self-Balancing Side-Shake Shoes.

New Compound Elevator Separators, with Outside Fans.

Counterbalanced Twin Shoe Elevator Separators.

Double End Aspirator Separators.

Perfected Milling Separators

Counterbalanced Milling Separators.

Latest Types fitted with Self-Oiling Chain Bearings, or Ball Bearings, Automatic Centrifugal Disc Dust-proof Eccentrics, Automatic Screen Self-Cleaning Device.

Built in 138 different types and sizes, with capacities varying from 30 to 6,000 bushels per hour.

S. HOWES CO. (A. C. BARBEAU)

A. GILLI, Manager,

64, Mark Lane, London, E.C. 3.

M1

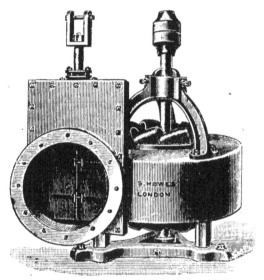

The British School of Milling

.. *and* ..

Laboratories of Cereal Chemistry

AYNSOME,

Director :
J. STEWART REMINGTON.

Nr. Grange-over-Sands,

Lancashire.

Full Courses in Milling, Flour Mill Chemistry, Baking and Fermentation, ✦ Mechanical Drawing and Bacteriology.

ANALYSES OF ALL
MILL PRODUCTS.

The Remington Process of Grain Testing, indispensible to Scientific Conditioning, and the production of uniform products.

FULL DETAILS ON APPLICATION.

Telegraphic Address : "PRIORY MILLS, CARTMEL,"

Keep DUST from your LUNGS

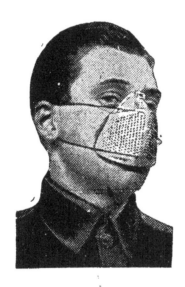

Write for Book No. 3 of
SAFETY APPLIANCES AND GOGGLES

SIMON'S AUTOMATIC
WEIGHERS

Spiral

Sack

Shoots.

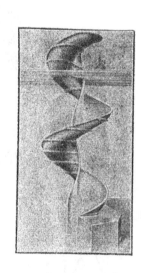

Richard Simon & Sons, Ltd.
NOTTINGHAM.

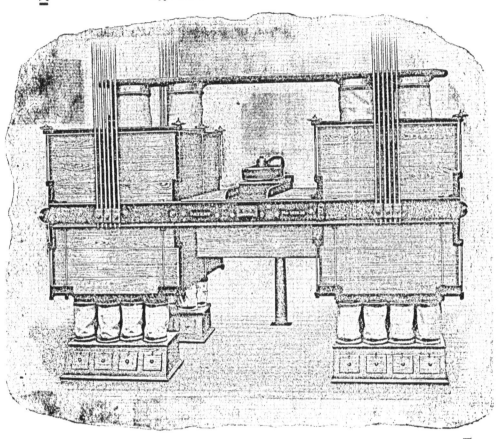

THE "BANBURY"

PATENT

WHEAT HYDROLIZER

AND CONDITIONER

THE Highest Natural and Scientific results in Milling and in the baking qualities of Flour are only to be obtained by this system.

SAMUELSON & CO.

LIMITED.

BANBURY.

Made in the USA
Coppell, TX
24 June 2020